The Life Cycle of the Soul.

Table of Contents

Welcome to the Life Cycle of the Soul

This gentle yet powerful workbook has been lovingly created to guide you on an inward journey through the sacred and timeless landscape of your soul's evolution. Life Cycle of the Soul is a spiritual invitation to explore the deeper dimensions of your being across lifetimes, through healing, and into awakening. Within these pages, you will be held and supported as you explore past life healing, soul retrieval, soul contracts, the Akashic Records, karmic cycles, and the in-between spaces of the spirit world. Whether you yearn for healing, seek clarity, or feel the call to remember who you truly are, this workbook is your companion and mirror. It offers a map to help you uncover who you have been, embrace who you are, and align with the highest version of who you are becoming. As a qualified Clinical Hypnotherapist, Regression Therapist, and Past Life & Life Between Lives Practitioner with nearly two decades of experience, I have had the profound honour of guiding thousands of souls through transformational healing journeys. Drawing from my extensive clinical training, spiritual practice, and years of soul work, this resource has been carefully crafted to offer you the same depth of healing and insight I provide in one-to-one sessions. This workbook is not just a tool but a sacred space, a spiritual ally, and a portal into your soul's wisdom. Through journaling prompts, guided meditations, therapeutic exercises, and spiritual teachings, you will begin to reclaim the forgotten pieces of yourself and integrate them into wholeness. You do not need to have prior experience with hypnotherapy or regression. You only need a willingness to listen deeply and meet yourself with love. Life Cycle of the Soul invites you to remember your essence whole, eternal, divinely guided and walk forward with courage, clarity, and grace along your sacred path.

Disclaimer and Self-Care Reminder

This workbook is designed for personal insight, spiritual reflection, and self-guided growth. It is not intended to diagnose, treat, or cure any psychological, emotional, or medical condition. The exercises within may bring up deep emotions or memories. Please practice self-care and seek support from a qualified mental health professional or therapist if needed. The author is a qualified hypnotherapist and regression practitioner. While every effort has been made to ensure the safety and integrity of this material, all activities are undertaken at the reader's own discretion and responsibility.

The Birth of a Soul

Source the origin, essence, and purpose of who you are.

The Soul Before Time

Before you had a name, you existed before the Earth knew your footprints or the stars knew your gaze. Not in a form, not in a body, not even as a personality but as a frequency, a spark, a consciousness. A soul. The soul is not born in time. It is not created in a hospital room or a womb. It does not arrive at the first heartbeat. The soul emerges from the very fabric of the Divine, birthed not in a moment but in a movement. A movement of love, of intention, of cosmic breath. We must look beyond biology and the mystical to understand the soul. While the body is temporal and decays, the soul is eternal, expanding beyond any lifetime. The immortal self, the true self, exists across dimensions and incarnations. It holds your blueprint, your truth, your sacred memory. Every human experience you've ever had is just one thread in a much greater tapestry woven by the soul over lifetimes. The you reading this now is the most recent expression of something vast, beautiful, and ancient.

What Is a Soul? Definitions Beyond the Material

We must begin by asking the question that underpins the entire spiritual journey: What is a soul? This is no simple task because the soul defies reduction. It cannot be measured, dissected, or contained. But it can be known. It can be felt. It can be remembered. The soul is the eternal essence of who you are. It is your true identity, untouched by fear or conditioning. While your personality is shaped by environment and experience, your soul is shaped by truth, purpose, and love. Your divine blueprint carries the memories, lessons, gifts, and wisdom from many lifetimes. A unique expression of Source, or the Infinite, individuated and sent forth to explore. The silent observer behind your thoughts and emotions, the one who watches without judgment. A living bridge between the spiritual and physical realms. An eternal traveller, journeying through realms, planets, dimensions, and human experiences to expand consciousness. You are not a body with a soul. You are a soul with a temporary body. And this soul, your soul, has never been "young." Even souls newly born from the Source carry ancient intelligence because they are created from the Infinite.

The Soul's Divine Origin

The soul is born not through biology but through emergence. It arises from Source, the boundless field of divine consciousness known as God, the All, the One, the Eternal Flame. From this field, infinite sparks of light are breathed into existence. These sparks of souls are not separate from the Source but are individuated within it. Like a drop of water in the ocean, they are made of the same essence yet travel outward to learn and experience. Why does Source send out these soul sparks? Not from lack or need, but from overflowing love. The Divine desires to experience itself through diversity. Each soul is a mirror through which the Infinite sees its face. Your soul is one of those sacred sparks, born from the love of the universe, given a vibration as unique as your fingerprint. This moment of emergence is not dramatic it is intimate. It is quiet, subtle, like the first glow of dawn. And yet, it is the most sacred moment in your existence: the beginning of your eternal becoming.

A Deep Dive into Definitions.

Let us begin at the foundation. What exactly is a soul? We hear the words " soulmates, soul journey, soul food, " and " soul purpose " often, but few pause to truly define them. To grasp its nature is to shift your understanding of who you are and why you are here.

Definition 1: The Eternal Essence.

The soul is your eternal essence. It is the aspect of you that existed before this life and will continue long after. It is not bound by time, space, culture, gender, or belief. It is you, without the story, trauma, or titles, pure, radiant, and whole.

Definition 2: The Divine Spark.

The soul is a spark of the Divine. It is a fragment of the Source of God, the Universe, and the Infinite Consciousness. Like a drop of water from an ocean, it contains the essence of the whole yet moves through creation as an individuated being. It is divinity exploring itself.

Definition 3: The Carrier of Memory and Purpose.

The soul carries memories not just of this life but of many. It holds the impressions of what you've learned, loved, suffered, created, and healed. These soul memories are woven into your intuition, tendencies, dreams, and deepest desires. The soul also carries purpose. You were not born by accident. Your soul came with intention.

Definition 4: The Observer and the Embodier.

Your soul is the silent observer of your life, the one who watches without judgment as you experience pain, joy, love, and loss. It is also the embodied experiencer, learning through contrast. It is both your teacher and your student.

Definition 5: The Bridge Between Worlds.

The soul is a bridge, a sacred channel between the spiritual and physical realms. It allows the infinite to express itself through the finite. The soul speaks through art, compassion, healing, intuition, and wisdom.

What we call 'death' is simply a doorway to the next chapter of our existence.

Elizabeth Kubler-Ross

The Soul's Nature: Unique and Yet Universal.

Every soul is unique. It cannot be replicated like a snowflake, a star, or a note in a divine melody. And yet, all souls are part of the same whole. This is the great paradox of the soul: it is both individual and interconnected. Both sovereign and divine. You are not merely a human being who happens to have a soul. You are a soul, first and foremost, currently experiencing human life. Understanding this shifts everything. It softens our suffering, deepens our compassion, and expands our vision. When we see each other as souls rather than roles, healing begins.

How Souls Are "Born": Emergence from Source.

The concept of "birth" implies a beginning. But the soul, in truth, has no beginning and no end. Still, for the sake of language, we describe its emergence. From the unmanifested field of pure consciousness, what mystics call Source, God, Spirit, the soul emerges as a spark of awareness. It is formed not by mechanics but by intention. A desire within the Divine to explore, express, and evolve. This emergence is not singular. Countless souls are birthed through divine will. Some are new, freshly formed. Others are ancient, seasoned by numerous journeys. Each carries a different rhythm, a different tone, a different task. Some are teachers, others are learners, healers, artists, destroyers of old systems, and bringers of truth. No soul is higher or lower, only on a different path. Some souls originate close to Earth, known as Earth Souls. Others come from realms far beyond, known as Star Seeds. Still others are what some call Wanderers—souls who travel between realms offering light, without a permanent home. Wherever your soul hails from, one truth remains: you chose to come here. And not by accident.

In between lives, we return to a place of unconditional love, review, and planning. It is from here that we choose our next path.

Dr Michael Newton, Journey of Souls

The Oversoul and the Soul Fractal

As the soul emerges from Source, it may do so not as a single entity but as a fractal, a more minor, individuated extension of a larger Oversoul. This Oversoul holds multiple expressions of itself, each exploring a different path, lesson, or dimension. As you are now, you are one unique expression of your Oversoul's wisdom-in-progress. This concept, taught in mystical, esoteric, and metaphysical traditions, helps us understand the complexity of the soul. While your current life feels central to your awareness, it is just one flame flickering in a much larger constellation. From the Oversoul's perspective, there is no separation. All aspects are loved, observed, and guided without judgment. What you experience here adds to the wisdom of the whole. While we often speak of "the soul" as singular, many mystical traditions describe it as a fractal. What you experience now is not the totality of your soul but a facet of a much larger being, your Oversoul. The Oversoul is like a great tree, and each incarnation is a branch. As you are now, you are one expression among many, each exploring different paths, lessons, and lifetimes, often simultaneously. Some traditions describe parallel incarnations happening across galaxies, timelines, or dimensions. These other selves are not strangers. They are you, evolving alongside you, all held in the heart of the Oversoul. When you experience sudden insight, déjà vu, or intuitive brilliance, it may be your Oversoul speaking, offering wisdom gathered from other lifetimes, other branches.

Soul Groups and Soul Families.

Souls do not emerge alone. They come forth in clusters of soul groups or soul families. These beings travel together across many incarnations, supporting one another's growth. You may change roles: mother becomes son, enemy becomes healer, lover becomes friend. But the soul recognises. Have you ever met someone and felt you've known them forever? Have you experienced an unexplainable comfort or tension with a stranger? These are signs of a soul contract. You've likely known them before. You chose to meet again. Soul families serve as mirrors, teachers, allies, and sometimes catalysts. Their purpose is never to harm but to provoke awakening. Sometimes, the greatest pain brings the most significant growth. Often, the most profound healing happens not in solitude but in relationship. Some souls travel with you, lifetime after lifetime. Others join briefly to spark a lesson or open a path. All encounters are sacred. All have meaning. Soulmates, twin flames, karmic ties, and divine partnerships are all examples of soul contracts within these families. They are not always easy. The souls who love you the most may play the most challenging roles because they agreed to help you grow. Have you ever met someone and felt an instant connection—or even a deep trigger? These are echoes of old agreements. Your soul remembers, even when your mind does not.

The Soul's Descent into Matter.

Once the soul has chosen its path, formed its agreements, and shaped its blueprint, it begins the journey into matter. This is what we call incarnation. Contrary to popular belief, the soul doesn't simply "drop in" at birth. The process is much more subtle and sacred. Many spiritual teachings agree that the soul begins to align with the physical body around the time of conception. It may weave in and out of the womb space, gently acclimating to Earth's energy, the lineage it has chosen, and the emotional frequency of the mother and father. The womb becomes a sacred gateway, a threshold between spirit and matter. During pregnancy, the soul may observe, prepare, and infuse its energetic imprint into the developing body. Some say the soul enters fully at the first breath, while others believe it gradually anchors into the body over several years. Regardless of the moment, the body is not merely flesh. It is a vessel of light, a temple of experience through which the soul will explore its lessons. The soul chooses everything: the time, the place, the family, and even the challenges. Nothing is random. All is selected for growth.

Why We Forget.

If we are souls of such divine intelligence, why do we forget who we are? This is one of the greatest spiritual paradoxes. Forgetting is not a flaw. It is part of the design. Earth is a realm of contrast. It is through forgetting that we are allowed to remember. Through darkness, we find our light. Through limitation, we discover our infinite nature. Through separation, we return to unity. We would not truly choose to awaken if we were fully aware of our soul's power, path, and origin. We would be programmed. The amnesia allows for free will. And through that free will, we rediscover ourselves with greater depth and authenticity. But the soul leaves breadcrumbs: dreams, intuition, synchronicity, and a longing we cannot name. These are sacred echoes, guiding us back to remembrance.

The Pre-Birth Planning Process.

Before incarnating, your soul returns to what is sometimes called the interlife—a space between lives where it rests, heals, and reviews. Here, in counsel with guides, elders, and members of your soul group, you prepare for your next journey. Nothing is imposed. You are never punished or assigned. Every choice is yours, guided by the soul's desire to evolve.

This preparation includes the crafting of your soul blueprint, a sacred map containing:

Life themes and core lessons.

The timing and place of your birth.

Your physical body, genetics, and heritage.

Soul contracts and relationships.

Planned challenges for growth.

Potential exit points (when you may choose to return to spirit).

Spiritual gifts, skills, and intuitive tools.

Choosing the Human Form.

Your soul selects your body as an artist chooses a canvas intentionally and with love. It chooses the genetic lineage, physical appearance, health predispositions, and energetic make-up that best support your purpose. Even bodies that face illness, disability, or difference are chosen for profound spiritual reasons. These are not limitations but sacred expressions of the soul's path. Your soul also chooses your family, not because they are perfect but because they will shape you. Parents, siblings, caretakers, and even those who cause pain are part of your soul's curriculum. Again, this is not about blame. The soul seeks growth, not comfort. And through contrast, it learns to embody its light more fully.

Incarnation: The Soul's Descent into Matter.

Once all is prepared, the soul begins its descent into physical reality. This descent is not a fall but a dance, a weaving. The soul gently integrates with the energy of the developing embryo, sometimes entering and withdrawing during pregnancy until fully anchored, often at birth, though sometimes earlier or later. Birth is traumatic for the body but sacred for the soul. It is the narrowing of infinite consciousness into a finite form. A temporary forgetting. A great risk. And yet, the soul comes willingly. You are here because you chose to be. You decided to experience emotion, duality, embodiment, and evolution. You chose Earth, this dense, beautiful, challenging realm, as your soul school. And you were brave to do so.

The Sacred Amnesia.

One of the most bewildering aspects of incarnation is spiritual amnesia, which is forgetting who we are, where we came from, and why we're here. But this forgetting is not a flaw. It is a design feature of Earth's spiritual curriculum. To grow through free will, we must forget. If we remembered our soul contracts, divine origin, and infinite nature, we would not face the same struggles, temptations, or heartache. We would not choose love over fear. We would know it. Forgetfulness creates the contrast needed for true awakening. But the soul leaves signs, dreams, synchronicities, intuitive nudges, déjà vu, and unexplainable longings. These are breadcrumbs leading us home.

Remembering Who You Really Are.

Spiritual awakening is the moment the soul begins to remember itself through you. It may start subtly: a longing, a question, a discomfort with the superficial. It may also be triggered by loss, illness, or transformation. But once begun, the soul's call cannot be silenced. You start to see life differently. You seek truth, depth, and purpose. You realise you are more than a name, a job, or a body. You are energy, essence, and eternal. As you remember, you reconnect with your inner guidance. Life becomes less about surviving and more about becoming. And you no longer feel alone because the soul knows it always has been, and always will be, part of something greater.

The Evolution of the Soul.

Souls evolve by experiencing contrast and returning to love. They expand not just by acquiring knowledge but by embodying it. A young soul may explore power, ambition, and survival. A mature soul begins to seek meaning, truth, and compassion. An old soul often serves as a healer, teacher, or guide, walking through life with quiet depth. But age is not everything. Some young souls hold extraordinary wisdom, and some old souls still struggle with grounding. Each soul's path is sacred and unique. Growth is spiral, not linear. You revisit themes, deepen lessons, and evolve through cycles of remembering. There is no finish line, only more profound love.

You Are the Soul You've Been Searching For.

You are not here by accident. You are not broken, behind, or lost. You are a soul in motion, a luminous being choosing experience, healing, and life. No matter how far you feel from your purpose or peace, your soul has never left you. It is waiting, watching, and guiding you back to yourself. Sometimes, you may lose connection, but your soul does not lose you. It cannot. It is you. You have never indeed been alone. The quiet ache you've felt in your chest, the yearning for something more, is the soul calling you home. It whispers in the spaces between distractions. It speaks through poetry, nature, music, and stillness. It echoes in déjà vu and stirs during sleepless nights. It reaches through dreams, signs, and strange synchronicities that defy logic. This sacred discomfort is the beginning of awakening. You are being invited to remember. You are being called not to become someone new but to return to who you've always been beneath the noise, the masks, and the fear.

This Is a Homecoming.

To live a soul-led life is not floating above reality or bypassing pain. It is to walk through the world with sacred awareness. To feel deeply. To choose with integrity. To speak from your centre. Offer your gifts not from your ego but from service. It is a path of devotion, not to dogma but to truth. To the living spirit that pulses within all things. When you reconnect with your soul, the outer world may not change immediately, but your relationship to it will. You begin to walk with intention. You become gentler with yourself. You hold space for others. You start to trust the unfolding. This is the path of remembrance. And it is the journey of a lifetime.

Closing Reflection.

If no one has ever told you before, let these words now be etched upon your heart:

You are not too late. You are not too much. You are not unworthy of peace or joy or love.

You are a soul on a sacred journey, braver than you know, wiser than you remember, and more powerful than you've been taught to believe. Everything you need is already within you, including every lesson, gift, and key. You came here equipped, ready. You are the soul you've been searching for. And this, this moment is your invitation to remember.

Soul Contracts & Sacred Agreements

Why do we choose our path before we walk it?

The Sacred Choice Before Birth.

Long before your first breath, your soul made choices. Not random decisions, but sacred ones. You didn't simply arrive you chose this life. You chose your body, your family, your challenges, your gifts. You chose the key people you would meet, the opportunities you would be drawn to, and the patterns you would work to transform. This may initially feel uncomfortable, especially if your life has been marked by difficulty. Why would any soul choose pain, hardship, or loss? The answer lies not in punishment but in purpose. The soul does not seek comfort; it seeks growth. It knows that in the fire of experience, it will remember who it truly is. It understands that love becomes real when it is chosen in the face of fear. Forgiveness becomes sacred when it is extended through pain. Strength is forged not in ease but in adversity. And so, before you arrived here, your soul sat in sacred council and shaped the outline of this life. You made agreements, not as obligations, but as intentions. You entered into contracts, not from control, but from conscious love.

What Is a Soul Contract?

A soul contract is an energetic agreement made before birth between souls who choose to meet in this life to help each other evolve.

These contracts can take many forms:

Family bonds that offer stability or challenge.

Friendships that uplift or trigger awakening.

Romantic relationships that catalyse transformation.

Brief encounters plant potent seeds of change.

Opponents or antagonists who reflect your deepest fears.

Each contract serves a spiritual purpose. Sometimes, that purpose is to support, heal, build, or love. Other times, it is to provoke, disrupt, expose, or free. None are accidental. Even the most painful relationships may have been forged in the most loving realms, made between souls who vowed to help each other remember who they are.

Pre-Birth Planning: Crafting the Soul's Blueprint.

Before incarnating, the soul enters the interlife, a realm of light, healing, and preparation. Here, with the assistance of spirit guides, councils, and higher-dimensional beings, the soul reviews its previous lives, examines karmic patterns, and prepares for its next journey. This sacred planning is infused with love, never obligation or punishment. Even when a soul agrees to experience trauma or limitation, it does so with deep intention, understanding that such experiences may unlock immense growth.

This process includes:

Choosing a soul family and key relationships.

Selecting core life lessons (e.g. courage, forgiveness, self-love).

Designing challenges and turning points.

Preparing potential exit points (when the soul may return home early).

Agreeing on the timing of awakening moments.

Reviewing gifts, wounds, and themes to carry forward.

Free Will and Destiny: The Dance Between Choice and Design.

One of the most beautiful truths about soul contracts is that they are fluid, not fixed. Nothing is "set in stone." Your soul sets a blueprint, but you are not bound to it. You can honour, modify, or even release a contract through free will once the lesson has been learned. Imagine your soul's plan as a landscape. There are mountains you choose to climb and valleys you decide to walk through. But how you move, when you pause, and who you meet on the trail are shaped by your choices. Fate brings the people and themes into your life. Free will determines how you respond. You may delay a lesson for years or master it in moments. You may walk away from a contract, only to revisit it later in a new form. You may even renegotiate soul contracts from the higher self through deep healing, prayer, ritual, or regression work. The universe is not rigid; it is responsive.

Your soul, the real you, is indestructible. It has lived before, and it will live again.

Dr. Michael Newton

Types of Soul Contracts

While every soul contract is unique, they often fall into familiar patterns. Understanding these can help you bring clarity and compassion to your relationships and life experiences.

Soulmates.

Soulmates are not limited to romance. A soulmate is any being with whom you share a deep soul resonance and a pre-agreed bond. They may be family, friends, lovers, or even pets. Some soulmates stay a lifetime. Others enter for a chapter. Either way, their purpose is to help you remember love.

Soulmates often bring:

Emotional safety.

Shared missions.

Healing presence.

Mutual growth.

Instant recognition.

Karmic Contracts.

These are the most complex and often the most difficult. Karmic contracts are born from unfinished business energetic imbalances carried over from past lives. These relationships usually feel magnetic, intense, and challenging to walk away from. These relationships are not meant to punish but to reveal. Once the karmic lesson is learned, the contract can dissolve or transform.

Karmic contracts can include:

Repeating conflict.

Power struggles.

Unresolved grief or betrayal.

Co-dependency.

Lessons in boundaries, self-worth, or forgiveness.

Twin Flames.

The twin flame concept describes a soul split into two incarnated expressions, each carrying a mirror of the other's wounds and light. This bond is not about romance or completion. It is about awakening. Twin flame contracts are often fiery, transformative, and spiritually catalytic. They trigger ego death, rapid evolution, and soul remembrance. Sometimes, they come together in partnership. Usually, they part after activation. The true purpose of the twin flame is not union with another but with your soul.

Sacred Teachers and Catalysts.

Some soul contracts are brief but powerful. A stranger who says the right thing at the right moment, a teacher who awakens your gifts, a relationship that lasts only weeks but shatters illusions—these are catalyst souls who agreed to deliver a key. They do not always stay, and their presence is not always peaceful, but their impact is profound.

The Sacred Purpose of Joy and Suffering

In Interlife, your soul chooses not just whom you will love but also how you will suffer. This can be a confronting truth. But from the soul's perspective, suffering is not cruelty but a container for transformation. These choices were not made to harm you. They were made to break the spell of forgetting. To push you back toward the soul. And you were not left to navigate them alone. The tools, timing, and inner strength needed to survive, and rise were also encoded within every contract.

You may have chosen:

A parent who withheld love to teach you self-worth.

A betrayal to teach you sovereignty.

A disability to teach compassion.

A loss to awaken your depth.

An abusive relationship reminds you of your power.

In the spirit world, we are not judged harshly. We are lovingly guided toward awareness and improvement.

Dr. Michael Newton

Signs You Are in a Soul Contract.

Wondering if a relationship or experience is part of a soul contract? Look for these clues:

Instant, intense connection (positive or negative).

A sense of familiarity or déjà vu.

A relationship that transforms you even through pain.

Repeating patterns that feel fated.

A sense that the relationship has a "mission".

Lessons that become clear only after time or distance.

An inability to "let go" until deep healing occurs.

Trust your intuition. Your soul always knows when something matters.

When Contracts Complete.

Just because a contract was made doesn't mean it's meant to last forever. Some are complete after a single conversation, while others may stretch over years or lifetimes.

Signs that a contract is complete:

The relationship no longer holds energy or charge.

The lesson has been integrated.

You feel peace or neutrality.

The karmic pull dissolves.

The person or pattern no longer triggers you.

Completion does not mean failure. It means graduation.

If you feel a contract ending, honour it with gratitude, even if it hurts. Release the soul with love. You may meet again in another form, another life, another dance.

Rewriting Your Soul Agreements.

While contracts are pre-birth decisions, they can be revisited and rewritten. Updating or releasing old soul agreements through conscious healing, intention, or spiritual work is possible.

Ways to do this:

Guided past life regression.

Akashic Record Sessions.

Sacred ritual and invocation.

Energy clearing or cord cutting.

Writing a soul letter to the person involved.

Speaking aloud your choice to release or revise the bond.

Your sovereignty is sacred. The soul is not a prisoner to its past but a co-creator of its future.

You Chose This for a Reason.

When life feels chaotic, painful, or unfair, it helps to remember: You chose this not as punishment but as purpose, not from weakness but from wisdom. Every person you meet, every challenge you face, and every longing you carry was chosen, agreed to, and designed to help you become more of your soul's truth. You are not behind. You are not broken. You are exactly where your soul intended you to be. If something no longer feels aligned, that is sacred information. You are not trapped in your old choices. You are always free to remember, re-align, and reawaken. This life is not a sentence. It is a sacred unfolding.

Closing Reflection.

You are not just living this life. You are weaving it, co-creating it, choosing it in every breath, with every thought, in every relationship. Your soul agreements are not burdens. They are bridges from fear to love, illusion to truth, separation to remembrance. And the more you walk them with awareness, the more light you bring to the world, not just your path but for those whose contracts include you. In the next chapter, we'll explore how the soul journeys across lifetimes, why we return, what we carry with us, and how echoes of previous lives may shape your current life. You are a soul in motion. You are the author of this sacred story. And the best is yet to unfold.

Spiritual growth comes from learning life lessons and fulfilling our purpose, not just in one lifetime but over many.

Dr. Michael Newton

The Souls Journey Through Lives

Time is the thread. The soul is the weaver

Beyond One Life.

The story you are living now is not your first and will not be your last. Your soul has walked many paths, worn many faces, spoken countless names. And though this current life may feel complete, it is one stanza in a much longer poem. The soul's journey is vast, intricate, and purposeful. It does not travel randomly or blindly. It evolves through experience, choice, and remembrance. To begin understanding your soul's journey through lifetimes is to lift the veil on who you indeed are. You are not only this moment, this body, or this history. You sum up many lives, loves, deaths, and awakenings.

The Purpose of Reincarnation.

Reincarnation is not simply the recycling of souls but the expansion of consciousness. It is the soul's way of deepening its wisdom, exploring new perspectives, balancing energy, and embodying love in all its forms.

Why would a soul choose to return again and again?

Because each life offers a unique classroom, you may learn to lead in one. In another, to serve. In one, to heal. In another, to forgive. Across lifetimes, you know about loss and loyalty, betrayal and compassion, freedom and fate. Reincarnation allows the soul to understand contrast. The poor soul understands wealth differently. The soul that has caused pain learns to heal. The soul who has walked in both light and shadow carries a more profound compassion into each new incarnation. Life is the soul's sacred school, and Earth is one of its most intense classrooms.

The Veil of Forgetting.

One of the great mysteries is why we do not remember our past lives consciously. Why begin again each time, in seeming ignorance? The answer lies in the power of the veil. Before each incarnation, the soul agrees to forget to pass through the veil of amnesia. This is not punishment but protection. It ensures that the soul can fully inhabit the new life without distraction or confusion from past timelines. Imagine trying to live this life while remembering a dozen past deaths, heartbreaks, or roles. The emotional weight would overwhelm most minds. The veil ensures you are present to what matters now and allows your soul's memories to filter through intuition, emotion, dreams, and deja vu gently. And yet, the soul never truly forgets. The memory remains encoded in your energy field, instincts, talents, fears, and longings.

Soul Memory in the Present Moment

Have you ever:

Felt a deep connection to a place you've never been?

Did you have a strong aversion or attraction to specific cultures, eras, or beliefs?

Excelled at a skill you never formally learned?

Experienced unexplainable phobias or health conditions with no known cause?

Did you meet someone and instantly feel like you've known them forever or met them in a dream?

These are echoes of past lives' soul memories rising to the surface.

Karmic Imprints and Lessons.

The soul carries with it not only lessons but imprints. These include karmic patterns, emotional residues, cellular memory, and spiritual gifts. Much of what we perceive as innate personality may be carried over from other lifetimes. This is why profound spiritual healing often involves work across timelines, not just this life's story but the stories beneath it. Karma is frequently misunderstood. It is not a divine punishment or a reward system. Karma is the energetic imprint of cause and effect, the soul's way of learning through experience. When you create imbalance in your lifetime through fear, violence, greed, betrayal, or suppression, your soul may experience the opposite in a future life, not to suffer but to understand. This re-balancing is not linear. It is conscious and intentional. These imprints are your soul's reminders: Here is where you have unfinished work. Here is where you are being asked to choose differently. Karma is not a sentence; it is a doorway to evolution.

Karmic imprints can look like:

Repeating relationship dynamics.

Inexplicable fears or anxieties.

Patterns of sabotage or self-denial.

Strong desires to serve, protect, or create.

Lifelong issues that defy logic or treatment.

Themes We Revisit.

Each soul carries archetypal patterns that thread through multiple lifetimes.

These themes may include:

Power and powerlessness.

Truth and illusion.

Love and abandonment.

Freedom and control.

Sacrifice and sovereignty.

Healing and wounding.

As you observe the repeating stories in your life, you will likely uncover your soul's themes. They are not here to torment you they are here to liberate you. Each time a theme returns, you meet it with new tools, more profound wisdom, and greater strength. Over time, your soul transforms it from a wound into a gift.

Soul Groups and Shared Journeys.

You are not journeying alone. Most souls travel in soul groups, clusters of beings who repeatedly incarnate in various roles to support and challenge one another's evolution. In one life, your soul group member may be your parent. In another, it may be your child, partner, mentor, or rival. The roles shift, but the contract remains: to catalyse growth and mirror the divine. These group journeys span thousands of years, multiple civilisations, and diverse expressions. You may even share specific missions or carry collective karmic wounds.

Recognising members of your soul group often brings:

Deep, instant recognition.

Emotional charge (positive or painful).

A sense of "destiny" or divine timing.

Significant life changes following the connection.

Soul groups are sacred alliances formed not out of convenience but cosmic design.

The Soul's Evolution Across Lifetimes.

Your soul is not static. Each lifetime, it evolves, growing more aware, expansive, and loving.

This evolution happens through:

Embodying virtues (compassion, courage, surrender, truth).

Integrating shadow aspects (jealousy, pride, shame, fear).

Honouring truth over illusion.

Living with intention and service.

Aligning with higher frequencies of love and wisdom.

Some lifetimes are "growth" lives filled with challenge, contrast, and awakening. Others are "rest" lives, quiet, gentle, and focused on healing or supporting others. Some are devoted to art, invention, magic, teaching, or justice. All are valuable. The soul does not rush. It honours timing. It returns only when it is ready and always with a purpose.

Past Lives and Present Gifts.

Your soul doesn't just carry wounds; it carries gifts. You may have cultivated healing skills, intuitive sight, leadership, creativity, spiritual power, or wisdom in other lives. These gifts lie dormant in your energy field until reactivated, often by circumstances, teachings, or spiritual awakening. Accessing these gifts is part of your soul remembering itself. They are here to support your purpose.

Signs of past life gifts include:

Natural abilities that feel effortless.

Magnetic attraction to specific tools or modalities.

Accelerated learning in spiritual work.

Vivid past life dreams or regressions.

Being told, "You've done this before."

Past Life Regression and Soul Healing.

Past-life regression is a powerful spiritual tool that allows the conscious mind to access soul memory. You can revisit lifetimes that hold keys to present challenges or gifts through gentle hypnosis or guided meditation.

These journeys can reveal:

The root of fears, phobias, or illness.

Unresolved trauma or karmic loops.

Forgotten soul agreements.

Hidden talents or soul missions.

Emotional clarity and deep healing.

Even simply witnessing a past life can begin to dissolve energetic blockages. It allows the soul to be seen, understood, and released from old roles. Regression is not just about curiosity; it is about completion.

Living a Soul-Integrated Life.

You are the culmination of many lifetimes. Every step you take now echoes with the wisdom of who you've been.

To live a soul-integrated life is to:

Honour your past, but do not be bound by it.

Choose consciously, knowing your choices ripple across time.

Recognise your patterns and alchemise them into power.

Heal not only for yourself but for your lineage and your soul group.

Embody your soul's frequency with grace and courage.

You are a soul in human form, not to escape humanity but to sanctify it.

Your soul's journey is not just "out there" it is happening now, in every moment, every breath, every decision to love more deeply.

Closing Reflection.

Your current life is sacred, but it is not all there is. You are the heir of many lifetimes, some triumphant, some tragic, and all meaningful. And within you lies the wisdom of the ages, waiting to be remembered. Honouring your soul's journey through life, you honour your whole self. You become the bridge between past and future, shadow and light, human and divine. In the next chapter, we will move between lifetimes, the space of rest, review, and reconnection. There, in the luminous halls of the spirit world, your soul remembers why it came, who it truly is, and where it is going next. You are not just living this life. You are weaving a legacy of light across the cosmos. And this life, right now, is your masterpiece in progress.

Our lives are not measured in years but in lessons learned, love given, and soul growth attained.

Wayne Dyer

The Interlife & Beyond

Where the soul returns to remember, rest, and realign

Beyond the Final Breath.

Death is not the end. It is a doorway. A release. A homecoming. To the soul, death is not a tragedy. It is not punishment, failure, or something to be feared. It is the gentle unravelling of the body's hold, the loosening of the veil, and the return to light. When the final breath is drawn, the soul rises not up, not out, but inward, toward its source. It slips from the confines of flesh like mist from water, free of pain and time, and once again aware of its eternal nature. What awaits beyond that moment is not darkness but love a love so vast, unconditional, and familiar that it is often met with tears of relief. The soul remembers: I am home.

The Life Between Lives (LBL) Space.

The space the soul enters after death is known by many names: the spirit realm, the between-lives state, the interlife. The soul is free beyond the pull of gravity and the veil of amnesia. This space is not a blank void it is a realm of light, sound, energy, and presence. It is vibrant with colour and movement. Souls are greeted by guides, loved ones, and members of their soul group. There is celebration, honouring, and reunion. In this space, the soul can see again. The density of Earth falls away, and the soul's frequency expands. Emotions become pure currents of energy. Thoughts are instant. Communication is telepathic. Love is the atmosphere. Time as we know it does not exist here. Everything is happening at once. The soul is not limited to a location it experiences rather than travels. This is not a static resting place. It is a vibrational dimension of healing, insight, and preparation.

The Return Home.

Upon arriving in the interlife, most souls are met by a familiar guide who has walked with them for many lifetimes. This guide is a companion, not a master, a presence of wisdom, not judgment. They often greet the soul with a message like, "Welcome back. You did well. Let's look at what you learned." There is usually a rest period, especially if the incarnation was intense or traumatic. The soul may spend time in healing chambers, energetic spaces where frequencies are rebalanced and wounds are soothed. These are not physical rooms but energy fields where loving light dissolves residual pain or distortion from the earthly body and experiences. Depending on its needs, the soul may sleep, drift, or exist in presence for moments or years. Healing in the interlife is gentle, non-linear, and complete.

The Life Review.

Once the soul is rested, it begins the life review, which is a profound, loving, and often emotional process of reflection. The soul views its most recent incarnation through a multidimensional lens. It sees its choices, relationships, intentions, and consequences from its perspective and through the eyes and hearts of others it affects. This is not punishment. There is no shame, no condemnation. The soul is surrounded by unconditional love. The purpose is awareness, not guilt. In many traditions and regression accounts, the review is supported by a council of wise, compassionate elders who help the soul integrate its journey. They ask thoughtful questions, offer gentle insight, and honour the soul's bravery. Every soul is celebrated for returning.

The soul may ask:

Did I live in alignment with my truth?

Where did I hold back?

Where did I love fully?

What did I learn?

What did I avoid?

Who did I impact?

Meeting the Soul Group.

After review, the soul often reconnects with its soul group and other beings it travels with across lifetimes. These are souls with whom we share deep resonance and purpose. Together, they may reflect on shared lives, laugh at the complexity of human experiences, and offer each other support. These reunions are often described as joyful, emotional, and transcendent. The soul group is not just a cluster of loved ones but a spiritual team, a collective of consciousness evolving in tandem. Some may have been your children, teachers, enemies, or partners. All are sacred companions. The soul remembers the bigger picture in the inner life: We chose this together. We are learning together.

The Spirit Guides and Soul Council.

Throughout your soul's journey, you are accompanied by one or more spirit guides beings of higher vibration who offer wisdom, protection, and direction. Some are with you across many lifetimes; others may appear for specific tasks. In interlife, these guides play a more active role. They may assist in:

Reviewing past life themes.

Helping the soul release attachments.

Guiding preparation for the next incarnation.

Supporting healing and reintegration.

Beyond the guides is the soul council, a group of elevated beings often described in LBL sessions as ancient, wise, and deeply loving. They do not command but inquire. They are not judges but stewards of evolution. This is sacred dialogue, not interrogation. It is a conversation between the soul and the Divine.

The soul council's role is to support clarity. They ask:

What did you wish to experience?

What did you learn?

What would you like to explore next?

Healing the Soul's Energetic Field.

Each incarnation leaves an energetic imprint. Joy, trauma, fear, love, and emotional residue can linger in the soul's field if not fully processed. This is not simply "rest." It is a refinement of frequency, allowing the soul to regain its full luminosity before re-entering the incarnation cycle. Many souls choose to wait multiple generations between lives to complete this deep restoration. In the interlife, the soul has access to profound energetic healing. This may involve:

Being bathed in frequencies of sound and colour.

Releasing etheric "scars" or density.

Calling back lost soul fragments.

Integrating shadow elements.

Clearing residual emotion from karmic experiences.

The Evolution of the Soul Between Lives.

Not all soul evolution happens in bodies. In the interlife, souls continue to:

Teach other souls.

Mentor younger beings.

Study cosmic laws.

Create in realms of light.

Travel through other dimensional spaces.

Participate in the divine orchestration of life.

Some advanced souls become guides for others. Some are called to help with transitions, which we know as death doulas or gatekeepers. Some choose to hold space for planetary healing or vibrational balance. Even between lives, the soul is in service, learning, and creation.

Preparing for the Next Incarnation.

With the help of guides and elders, the soul reviews potential timelines, families, cultures, and bodies. It studies probabilities, not certainties, and intuitively senses the right path. Some souls return quickly. Others wait. The timing is never forced. The next life must serve the soul's evolution, not its ego.

Once healing is complete and the soul feels ready, it begins preparation for its next incarnation.

This is an intentional and sacred process. The soul considers:

What lessons are in the soul's curriculum?

What energies are unresolved?

What qualities do we wish to be embodied?

Which gifts are ready to be activated?

What service does the soul feel called toward?

Choosing the Body, Family, and Blueprint.

Nothing is random. Even chaotic lives are often chosen for the precise alchemy they create. The soul does not seek ease. It seeks meaning. It selects circumstances that will best support the evolution of its frequency. The soul chooses:

The physical body – including health predispositions, gender, appearance, and limitations.

The family and lineage often select dynamics that reflect or trigger lessons and patterns.

The geographic location and culture – aligned with karmic themes or soul missions.

The blueprint – a life map with key contracts, challenges, and exit points.

The Descent Back to Earth.

When all is ready, the soul begins its descent into form. This sacred compression moves from light into density, from all-knowing to forgetting. As it merges with the developing embryo, the soul may move between realms, gradually adapting to the earthly vibration. It watches, feels, and prepares. The womb becomes a gateway. Birth is not the beginning it is the re-entry. As the soul takes its first breath, it forgets not who it is but how to speak it. The journey of remembering begins again.

Closing Reflection.

The interlife is not a fantasy. It is the forgotten realm that your soul calls home. You have been there before. You will return. And within you now, at this very moment, are the echoes of that place: peace, clarity, love, remembrance. When you touch stillness. When you dream vividly and feel something greater watching over you, the interlife reaches through the veil. You are more than your body. More than your story. More than this one life. You are a soul who has loved, lost, healed, guided, served, remembered, and returned many times. The next chapter will explore how the soul recovers across lifetimes through retrieval, shadow work, and profound transformation. Because sometimes, even souls carry wounds.

And all wounds, even the deepest ones, are portals to light.

The day science begins to study non-physical phenomena, it will make more progress in one decade than in all the previous centuries of its existence.

Nikola Tesla

The Soul's Blueprint & Higher Purpose

You were designed with intention and sent with purpose

The Map Within.

From the moment your soul emerged from Source, a unique blueprint was woven into its essence, a sacred pattern holding your soul's frequency, themes, gifts, desires, and intentions across time. This is not a rigid contract or predetermined fate. It is a living, breathing design, flexible enough to honour free will, yet specific enough to call you home when you drift. Your soul's blueprint is the divine architecture of your being. It contains the seeds of your highest potential, the qualities you came to embody, the lessons you explored, the people you met, and the difference you came to make. Discovering your blueprint is not binding yourself to a narrow path but finally hearing the song you were always meant to sing.

What Is a Soul Blueprint?

A soul blueprint is the energetic map created before incarnation. It outlines your life themes, soul contracts, key challenges, spiritual gifts, and higher calling in this lifetime.

Think of it as:

A compass guiding you toward meaning and growth.

A script, loosely written, allowing improvisation and choice.

A vibrational imprint carried in your energy field, voice, dreams, and desires.

A soul mission, encoded with love and wisdom from your higher self.

Your soul blueprint is not something you figure out intellectually. It's something you feel. It lives in the body, whispers through intuition, and resonates like a bell when you touch something true. You've known it since before you could speak. You feel it in moments of awe, the work you're drawn to, and the people who awaken something ancient in you. It reveals itself in dreams, synchronicities, and callings you cannot explain.

Life Purpose vs Soul Purpose.

Many people confuse life purpose with soul purpose. But they are not the same. Life purpose is how you express your soul's energy in this lifetime. It may change with age, growth, or environment. It's your mission to be a form teacher, healer, artist, parent, leader, and advocate. A soul's purpose is more profound. It is the essence of who you are and why you exist. It is what you came here to remember, embody, and radiate. It transcends any single life or role. For example, your life purpose may be to write books. Your soul purpose may be to illuminate truth, inspire awakening, or heal through words. You feel powerful, energised, and guided when the two are aligned. When they are not, you may feel lost even if everything looks "successful" on the outside. The goal is to let your life become the vessel for your soul's essence.

The Soul's Higher Calling.

Every soul carries a higher calling, its most profound desire to embody a particular quality or bring healing to a particular theme. Your higher calling is not necessarily "big" in worldly terms. It may not require a stage or a platform. Some of the most powerful souls quietly fulfill their purpose by loving well, choosing peace, tending gardens, and holding space for others to rise. The soul is not interested in how impressive your life looks. It cares only about how aligned it feels.

Some souls are called to:

Anchor light in dark places.

Break generational cycles.

Uplift consciousness through art or sound.

Teach spiritual truths through simple living.

Create sanctuaries of peace or joy.

Catalyse growth in others through challenge.

Carry ancient wisdom into modern times.

Remember and share love in all things.

How We Choose Our Blueprint.

Before incarnation, in the interlife space, the soul sits with its guides and council to shape its blueprint. The soul does not fear challenge. It understands that pressure creates diamonds. And it knows there will be help seen and unseen even in difficulty. Together, they reflect on:

Past life patterns that need balancing or healing.

Lessons that remain unfinished.

Contracts with other souls to meet again.

These are gifts that are ready to be activated.

Challenges that will catalyse growth.

Environments that will support evolution.

Timing, geography, ancestry, and collective energy.

With clarity and love, the soul chooses its path not to be tested but transformed.

Destiny, Divine Timing, and Free Will.

One of the most elegant aspects of the soul's blueprint is the dance between destiny and free will. Certain events, people, or experiences will likely happen, set in motion by prior soul contracts or karmic imprints. These are your destined moments: the crossroads, awakenings, and "chance" meetings that shift your course. But you still choose. How you respond to those moments, what you learn from them, and what you create after they are yours to shape. Divine timing often weaves through these intersections. You may not be able to force a door open before it's time, but when you're ready, life will meet you there. Your free will can delay but not destroy your soul's deeper becoming. The blueprint may bend and adapt, but it will continue whispering until you listen.

Recognising the Soul's Voice.

Your soul speaks through subtle yet persistent channels. To follow your blueprint, you must learn to tune in. Your soul does not judge. It guides with compassion. And it always allows you to return home.

Signs that you are aligned with your blueprint:

A deep sense of inner peace or "rightness".

Synchronicities are appearing often.

A pull toward certain people, places, or practices.

Recurring dreams, symbols, or visions.

Sudden clarity or spiritual downloads.

Physical vitality and energy when living your truth.

The quiet joy of doing what you were born to do.

Signs you're off-course:

Prolonged fatigue, disconnection, or dissatisfaction.

Repeating challenges or blockages.

Feeling invisible or unheard.

A sense of being lost, numb, or stuck.

External success that feels hollow.

The Blueprint Awakens in Stages.

Most people don't awaken to their blueprint all at once. It unfolds in layers, often through cycles of challenge, healing, and transformation. In early life, you may feel "different" or misunderstood. In your 20s or 30s, you begin questioning your path or feeling an inner unrest. In your 30s–50s, major career, relationships, health, and loss shifts may shake your identity and awaken your more profound truth. Later in life, you begin teaching, guiding, or embodying your wisdom in service to others. Awakening is not a straight line. It is a spiral. You revisit the same themes at deeper levels until you've fully integrated the lesson. Every soul has its own pace. Trust yours.

When Purpose Feels Elusive.

There are times when your soul's purpose may feel far away. You may be in a job that stifles you, a relationship that confuses you, or a life that feels disconnected from what you came to do.

In these moments, it's essential to:

Return to stillness.

Reconnect with your inner voice.

Ask your soul: What wants to emerge through me now?

Follow the next right feeling, not the perfect plan.

Purpose is not a destination. It is a way of being.

It often hides in the small things: how you listen, love, and show up.

The soul rarely shouts. It nudges. It waits. It trusts that you'll find your way when you're ready.

And you always do.

Living in Alignment.

To live your soul's blueprint is to live in alignment. This means:

Speaking your truth, even when it shakes.

Honouring your gifts, even when they feel strange.

Releasing what no longer resonates, even when it hurts.

Walking with courage, even when the path is unclear.

It is not about being perfect. It is about being present. Awake. Willing to grow.

When you live in alignment:

Life flows more easily.

The right people appear.

You feel energised, even during hard work.

Your intuition sharpens.

Opportunities arise organically.

You feel part of something greater.

You stop striving. You start remembering.

Sacred Contracts Within the Blueprint.

Your soul's design includes contracts with others who will play pivotal roles in your awakening.

These may include:

Mentors who activate your gifts.

Challengers who force you to set boundaries.

Partners who help you experience sacred union or karmic release.

Strangers who deliver messages.

Children become your greatest teachers.

Students who call forth your mastery.

Not all contracts last forever. Some are brief. Others are lifelong. Each is essential.

When you honour these contracts with grace, even when they end, you honour your soul's growth.

Co-Creating with the Universe.

Living your soul's blueprint does not mean surrendering control. It means co-creating dancing with the Divine in complete awareness. You set intentions, take aligned action, and trust the unfolding. You don't force your path; you follow it, even when it winds through unexpected terrain. Miracles come when action and alignment meet. And when you truly begin living from your blueprint, your life becomes:

A living prayer.

A sacred offering.

A beacon for others seeking their way.

You become a person with a purpose and a purpose embodied in a person.

Closing Reflection.

Your soul came here for a reason. Not to prove your worth but to express your truth. Not to chase success but to embody love. Do not follow someone else's map, but remember your own. You are not here by accident, and you are not off course. Even your detours are part of the design. The call you feel in your bones, the ache for something more, is your blueprint awakening. Your higher self asks: Are you ready to live what you came here for? And the answer, even if whispered, is already within you. In our final chapter, we'll explore how everything we've discussed reincarnation, soul healing, and sacred purpose intertwines in a more excellent cycle of evolution, service, and love. The soul's journey is not only personal; it is part of the collective awakening of all beings.

Collective Awakening of the Soul

You are not awakening alone

A Shift in the Winds.

There is a stirring in the world. A quickening. A rising. Perhaps you've felt it, the sense that something is changing. The old ways no longer work. That time is accelerating, truths are surfacing, and humanity stands on the edge of something vast and unknown. This is not your imagination. It is not chaos without meaning. It is the beginning of what mystics and seers have long foretold: the awakening of collective consciousness. And at the centre of it all is the soul, your soul, our souls, the soul of humanity itself, remembering its light and rising into new alignment.

What Is the Collective Awakening?

The collective awakening refers to the global spiritual reactivation occurring across the Earth, a mass remembrance of truth, unity, and divine connection. For generations, humanity has lived in a state of spiritual amnesia, rooted in separation, fear, materialism, and illusion. But beneath the surface, the soul has always been present, quietly guiding. As more individuals awaken to their soul's truth, a ripple is created in an energetic field that lifts others, opens hearts, and cracks old paradigms. This is not an accident. It is a designed moment in time, chosen by countless souls who agreed to return now to heal themselves and be way showers for a sleeping world. If you are reading this, you are likely one of them.

The Role of Old Souls and Light Bearers.

You may have always felt a little different. Perhaps you were the sensitive one, the truth-seeker, the one who questioned, the one who felt the world's pain too deeply. This is not a flaw. It is your frequency. You are what many would call an old soul who has lived many lifetimes, carried wisdom across time, and chosen to incarnate now for a purpose.

Old souls often:

Awaken early in life or through sudden spiritual shifts.

Struggle with dense systems or superficial living.

Feel a deep longing for home, truth, or unity.

Carry natural healing or intuitive abilities.

Have a strong inner compass and sense of justice.

Are drawn to teach, guide, create, or heal.

You did not come to fit in. You came to light the way.

The Earth as a Living Soul.

Just as each human has a soul, so too does the Earth. Our planet is not a lifeless sphere but a conscious, sentient being with cycles, energy centres, and wisdom. Indigenous traditions have long known this, calling her Gaia, Pachamama, or Mother Earth. She is more than our environment. She is our spiritual partner. As humanity awakens, so too does the Earth. And as she shifts through climate, frequency, and collective upheaval, she mirrors our inner changes. We are not separate from the Earth. Her healing is our healing.

The Soul's Service to the Whole.

In previous chapters, we explored the soul's journey as an individual path—through birth, life, death, healing, and purpose. But now we arrive at the more profound truth:

Your soul is not here for you alone.

Yes, your healing matters. Yes, your path is sacred.

Everything you awaken within yourself becomes part of the collective field.

When you forgive, the frequency of forgiveness becomes more accessible to others.

When you live with integrity, truth is strengthened in the human grid.

When you reclaim your light, you help dissolve collective shame.

When you heal your ancestral wounds, you liberate your bloodline.

When you speak your truth, you permit others to do the same.

You are a node in a great web, and every act of love, courage, or presence strengthens the whole.

Healing the Collective Shadow.

Just as individuals carry wounds, so too does humanity. We are now being asked to face and heal the collective shadow of centuries of fear, oppression, inequality, disconnection, and abuse. This is why old systems are crumbling, why truths are surfacing. Why so many feel ungrounded, anxious, or overwhelmed. We are in a planetary night of the soul a sacred unravelling, not to destroy us, but to awaken us. The soul's role is not to bypass this shadow but to walk through it with light. To bring presence to pain. To hold vision where others hold fear. To be midwives of the new world, even as the old dissolves.

Anchoring the New Frequency.

As the collective awakens, a new frequency is anchoring into the Earth. This new paradigm does not arrive through governments or technology. It is birthed through the human heart, through the soul remembering itself and choosing to live in truth. You carry this frequency. You are not just here to witness the shift; you are part of it. It is not built on power, control, or dominance, but on:

Compassion.

Co-creation.

Authenticity.

Interconnection.

Reverence for all life.

Alignment with natural rhythms.

Practical Ways to Serve the Awakening.

You don't need a title or a stage to contribute. Every soul has a role in the unfolding. Here are sacred ways to serve the collective awakening:

Live with integrity. Align your inner values with your outer actions.

Speak with love. Words create worlds. Use yours to uplift.

Create with purpose. Let your art, business, parenting, or service carry light.

Hold space for others. Presence is the most potent healer.

Trust your intuition. The soul speaks softly but clearly. Follow its guidance.

Care for your body and the Earth. They are not separate. Treat both with reverence.

Keep learning. Your growth helps others rise.

Remember your mission. You are here on purpose, for a purpose.

Each act of soul alignment is a prayer for the world.

The Rise of Soul-Led Communities.

As more souls awaken, new forms of community emerge, not based on hierarchy or conformity but on shared resonance. You may be called to find or create one of these communities. If so, follow that call. The soul thrives in connection. We are not meant to do this alone. We are remembering together.

These are:

Circles of healing.

Sanctuaries of remembrance.

Spiritual networks across the globe.

Families of choice, bonded by soul.

Collaborative projects rooted in consciousness.

The Global Soul Pulse.

Beneath the noise of media, politics, and fear, something ancient is rising: a global pulse, a rhythm of awakening that can be felt in meditation, silence, music, and the natural world.

This pulse is calling us to:

Slow down.

Listen deeply.

Honour the sacred in everyday life.

Live as stewards, not consumers.

Make choices with consciousness.

Remember our shared humanity.

It is no longer time to sleep. It is time to embody the soul in full.

The Future Is Soul-Led.

We stand at a turning point as individuals and as a species. The choice before us is not technological, political, or economic. It is spiritual. It is a question of identity: Will we continue as forgetful humans or rise as awakened souls? The future is not written. It is being co-created by every choice we make now. You are not too small. You are not too late. The soul is not measured by size but sincerity; every act of truth matters. Every act of love transforms. The more you remember, the more you inspire remembrance in others.

Final Reflection.

Dear soul, you are not broken, lost, or alone. You are ancient and luminous. You are part of something extraordinary. In doing so, you become a living bridge between the worlds, a radiant expression of Source walking the Earth and reminding others that they, too, are divine. Your soul is the medicine the world has been waiting for. And this awakening is only the beginning.

You came here for this moment.

You chose to awaken.

You chose to heal.

You chose to rise.

Soul Healing

You are not broken. You are becoming whole

When the Soul Fractures.

The soul, though eternal and luminous, is not immune to pain. While its essence cannot be destroyed, it can become wounded, dimmed, or fragmented by intense human experiences. Trauma, grief, betrayal, loss, abuse, suppression, and disconnection from one's truth can create energetic imprints that remain long after the experience has passed. These wounds affect the body or mind and imprint on the soul. And when a soul is deeply overwhelmed or endangered, it may respond in a profoundly protective way: by fracturing. This is not failure. It is intelligence. Just as the body goes into shock to survive physical trauma, the soul may disperse part of its energy, a fragment of its consciousness, to keep itself safe. This is what we call soul loss. This is recognised as a natural consequence of profound suffering in shamanic traditions. With awareness, it is not permanent. What is lost can be returned, and what is fragmented can be retrieved. What was once hidden can be lovingly brought back into the light.

Signs of Soul Loss.

Most people live unaware that parts of their soul have been left behind in earlier moments of pain or disempowerment. Yet the symptoms are often present, quiet, persistent echoes of something missing. You may not know what has been lost, but your soul remembers. And the longing to become whole again is the call of your soul asking to return to itself.

Common signs of soul loss include:

A sense of numbness or emotional flatness.

Feeling detached from life, as though watching from a distance.

Depression or grief that feels disproportionate or without apparent cause.

Difficulty forming or maintaining deep connections.

Addictive behaviours are used to fill an unnamed emptiness.

Memory gaps, especially around trauma.

Chronic fatigue or spiritual exhaustion.

A haunting sense that "something is missing" or "I am not all here".

What Causes Fragmentation?

Soul fragmentation can occur at any time, especially during formative or emotionally intense moments. In each case, part of the soul may "step out," separating to avoid being fully engulfed by pain. That part may remain frozen in time and be waiting to be retrieved. These may include:

- Childhood trauma, such as neglect, abuse, or abandonment.
- Sudden loss of a loved one, particularly in childhood or adolescence.
- Shaming or suppressing authentic expression.
- (e.g. being told your voice, art, feelings, or spiritual gifts are "wrong").
- Accidents or surgeries, especially those involving unconsciousness.
- Emotional betrayal by someone deeply trusted.
- Spiritual disillusionment, such as betrayal by a teacher, community, or faith.
- Witnessing violence or experiencing war, natural disaster, or collective trauma.
- Past-life trauma was carried forward unresolved.

What Is Soul Retrieval?

Soul retrieval is the sacred process of calling back these lost or fragmented parts of the self. This is not about revisiting trauma for trauma's sake. It is a healing journey guided by love, reverence, and patience. It allows the soul to become whole again, not just to remember who it was but to reclaim its light, power, creativity, joy, and sense of purpose. In traditional cultures, soul retrieval was performed by shamans, priestesses, or seers. The practitioner would journey through non-ordinary reality, often guided by drums, breath, or plant medicine, to find the lost soul part, communicate with it, and invite it home. Regardless of the method, the intention is to lovingly invite home what has been lost, hidden, or silenced.

In modern contexts, soul retrieval may also happen through:

Hypnotherapy or regression.

Guided meditation.

Energy healing.

Deep inner child work.

Dreamwork or visioning.

Ritual and ceremony.

Spontaneous awakening experiences.

Meeting the Lost Parts.

Your role is not to "fix" them but to witness them with love, listen with compassion, and offer safety. Sometimes, all a lost part needs is to be seen.

When we approach our fragmented soul parts, we often discover they are:

Younger versions of us - child-like, confused, or scared.

Frozen in time, still reliving the moment of trauma.

Holding specific emotions, rage, grief, shame, fear, or longing.

Guarded and afraid to return because they fear being hurt again.

Carrying gifts, creativity, confidence, playfulness, sensuality, or spiritual power.

Each part has a voice. A story. A need.

The Integration Process.

Calling a soul part back is only the beginning. True healing happens in integration.

This means:

Creating inner space for the part to return

Offering it what it didn't receive the first-time validation, care, protection

Rebuilding trust with the self

Adjusting your life to honour the needs and gifts of this part

Allowing your energy to shift and expand

Integration is not always immediate.

It may feel disorienting, emotional, or even physically intense.

Old memories may rise, and new insights may surface.

Be gentle. You are not regressing—you are reclaiming. And what returns will change you.

Shadow Work: The Soul's Other Half.

Soul retrieval is often accompanied by shadow work, which is facing the parts of ourselves we have disowned, repressed, or judged. The shadow is not "bad." It is simply what we were taught to hide. But it does not disappear. It lives in our bodies, reactions, and relationships until we bring it to light. Healing the soul means calling back the beautiful parts and embracing the whole self, shadow and all. In doing so, we move from fragmentation to integration. From shame to sovereignty.

These may include:

Anger or rage.

Sexuality.

Envy or pride.

Fear of power or visibility.

Deep vulnerability.

Spiritual gifts suppressed by shame.

Healing the Soul Across Lifetimes.

Some soul wounds stretch beyond this life. They echo from past lives where trauma, fear, guilt, or grief was never resolved.

These wounds may show up as:

Chronic health issues with no medical explanation.

Phobias or anxieties that feel irrational.

Blocks in abundance, love, or creativity.

Patterns of martyrdom, persecution, or powerlessness.

A deep fear of being seen, heard, or using one's gifts.

Past-life healing is often needed to retrieve soul fragments left behind in other timelines.

This may involve:

Past life regression.

Akashic records work.

Ritual forgiveness.

Energetic release ceremonies.

Rewriting the narrative with the wisdom of the higher self.

When we heal across timelines, the shifts in this life are profound. The soul no longer drags its past; it walks freely, guided by present light.

Rituals and Sacred Practices for Soul Healing.

Healing the soul is sacred work. It deserves ceremony. Here are some ways to support the journey:

1. **Create a Soul Altar.**

Include photos, candles, crystals, or symbols that connect you to your essence. Sit with it regularly and speak to your soul.

2. **Write to Your Lost Parts.**

Journal letters to your inner child, younger self, or unknown fragments. Invite them home. Tell them they are safe now.

3. **Guided Meditation Journeys.**

Visualise a sacred space within. Ask your soul parts to come forward. What do they need? How do they feel? Listen deeply.

4. **Elemental Rituals.**

Use fire to release old pain. Use water to cleanse. Use earth to anchor. Use air to speak affirmations into being.

5. **Voice Vibration.**

Speak your truth aloud. Toning, chanting, or mantras can vibrate your body and energy field.

6. **Call on Guides and Ancestors.**

Ask for support from your spirit team. They are present and willing to assist your healing.

Everything you need to know is within you. The secrets of your past lives, your soul's purpose, and your destiny are waiting to be unlocked.

Sonia Choquette

Living as a Whole Soul

The goal of soul healing is not perfection; it is wholeness. You will still have emotions and be human, but you will no longer feel scattered, hollow, or disconnected from your truth. You move from survival to sovereignty, from forgetting to remembrance, from wounding to wisdom. You walk the world not as a seeker but as a soul fully embodied.

When you are whole, you:

Know your worth without external proof.

Make choices that align with your soul's wisdom.

Attract relationships that honour your light.

Express yourself authentically.

Feel the presence of your soul in everyday life.

Closing Reflection.

You were never broken, and you were never less than. You were missing pieces of yourself that got left behind along the way. But now, you are calling them back. And as they return bit by bit, breath by breath, you begin to remember the truth:

You are sacred. You are whole. You are home.

In the next chapter, we'll step beyond the individual journey and look at the soul's greater design, blueprint, destiny, and higher purpose. You are not only healing for yourself. You are awakening a deeper current within the tapestry of all life. You are becoming the soul you were always meant to embody.

Our lives are like a tapestry. The threads of past lives are woven into the present, creating a pattern of karma, destiny, and free will.

Carol Bowman

Soul Retrieval

Restoring Wholeness and Reclaiming Your Power

What is Soul Retrieval?

Soul retrieval is a shamanic and spiritual healing practice aimed at recovering lost fragments of a person's soul that may have separated due to trauma, emotional distress, or significant life events. This concept is deeply rooted in indigenous and shamanic traditions, where it is believed that when a person experiences profound emotional or physical trauma, a part of their soul may fragment and dissociate as a protective mechanism. These lost fragments do not disappear entirely but become disconnected from the conscious self, often remaining in the energetic realm or attached to specific events, locations, or even people. This phenomenon is commonly referred to as soul loss, which can result in feelings of emptiness, depression, disconnection, or a sense that something is missing from one's life. Soul retrieval is journeying into the spiritual or subconscious realms to locate and reintegrate these lost aspects, returning them to the person's energy field so they may feel whole again.

What is Soul Loss? – How Trauma Fragments the Soul.

Soul loss is a spiritual and energetic condition that occurs when a part of an individual's essence or life force becomes disconnected due to trauma, shock, or prolonged emotional suffering. This is not the loss of the soul in its entirety but rather a fragmentation, a protective mechanism in which parts of the self retreat or "hide" to shield against pain that is too overwhelming to process at the time. These parts often carry the memory of the trauma and become frozen in that moment of distress. From a spiritual perspective, soul loss may feel like emptiness, chronic fatigue, disconnection, numbness, or the sense that something is "missing" or "off." It can also manifest as persistent patterns of self-sabotage, difficulty forming healthy relationships, anxiety, or depression. The soul fragments may remain lost or hidden until consciously retrieved and reintegrated through healing practices such as shamanic soul retrieval, regression therapy, deep inner child work, or energy healing. By recovering these lost parts of the self, a person can feel whole again, restoring vitality, clarity, and a renewed sense of purpose.

Understanding Soul Loss.

Soul loss can occur due to various life experiences, including the following:

- Childhood trauma (abuse, neglect, abandonment).
- Loss of a loved one (grief, unresolved emotions).
- Physical or emotional abuse.
- Accidents or injuries that shock the system.
- Major life changes (divorce, relocation, career shifts).
- Toxic relationships or energetic entanglements.
- Betrayal and heartbreak.
- Suppression of emotions or forced conformity and repressed past life trauma.

Soul Loss, its causes and effects.

Soul loss is a spiritual and energetic phenomenon in which an individual loses fragments of their essence due to emotional, physical, or psychological trauma. This concept, found in many shamanic and indigenous traditions, suggests that when we endure severe distress or shock, a part of our soul or life force detaches as a survival mechanism. While this process can help us cope in the short term, prolonged soul loss may lead to feelings of emptiness, disconnection, and emotional numbness. Over the following few pages, we explore common causes of soul loss and how they impact an individual's well-being.

Symptoms of Soul Loss – Emotional Numbness, Chronic Fatigue, Feeling Disconnected.

Soul loss often manifests in subtle yet deeply unsettling ways. One of the most common symptoms is emotional numbness, a sense of detachment from life, where a person feels disconnected from their emotions, relationships, or purpose. It's as if the vibrant colours of life have dulled, and one can go through the motions without truly feeling anything. This numbness may be mistaken for apathy or depression, but it often stems from unresolved soul wounding.

Another hallmark is chronic fatigue, mainly when medical explanations fall short. This is the exhaustion of carrying unresolved spiritual and emotional weight. When vital energy is fragmented or missing, the person feels energetically depleted, unmotivated, or constantly tired, even after rest.

A third symptom is disconnection from the self, others, and the world. Individuals may feel like they are not fully "here," like a part of them is lost, stuck in the past, or waiting to return. This can lead to loneliness, emptiness, or searching for something they can't quite name. These symptoms are the soul's quiet cry for healing, integration, and the return to wholeness.

We learn wisdom from failure much more than from success. We often discover what will do, by finding out what will not do.

Dr. Michael Newton

Healing Ancestral and Collective Wounds – Carrying Family and Cultural Karma.

Ancestral and collective wounds are the emotional, energetic, and karmic imprints passed down through generations, often carried unconsciously within the soul's memory and the body's cellular structure. These wounds are not always our own, yet we experience them as inherited pain patterns of fear, shame, silence, unworthiness, or emotional burden that echo from our parents, grandparents, and ancestors before us. Likewise, collective wounds arise from the shared traumas of humanity wars, colonisation, persecution, and systemic oppression, leaving a lingering imprint in the collective psyche that affects our spiritual evolution and soul contracts. When these ancestral or collective traumas go unacknowledged, they can silently influence our lives in the form of repeating patterns, chronic emotional blocks, mysterious illnesses, or relationship struggles. From a spiritual perspective, your soul may have chosen to incarnate into a particular lineage to heal, transmute, and evolve the inherited energy within that bloodline. This is the sacred role of a spiritual bridge-builder or "wound-bearer" who heals not only for oneself but for generations past and future.

Healing these wounds begins with awareness and compassion. We release the energetic imprints of pain, shame, or limitation through intentional practices such as ancestral rituals, journaling, guided meditation, regression therapy, and Akashic record work. Soul retrieval and cord-cutting ceremonies may also free oneself from ancestral entanglements while honouring the wisdom and resilience of those who came before. You accept and liberate your lineage as you release what no longer belongs to you. You become the one who breaks the cycle. In doing so, you create space for new generational blessings to flow, restoring harmony within yourself and throughout your ancestral line and the collective consciousness. This healing is one of the most extraordinary acts of love you can offer to yourself, your descendants, and humanity.

People are not afraid of dying; they are afraid of not having lived. Past life memories remind us that we have lived before and will live again.

Dolores Cannon

How Trauma Can Affect the Soul

Trauma is stored in the body and mind and reverberates deeply through the soul. When a person experiences intense fear, shock, betrayal, or grief, especially sudden or overwhelming, a part of the soul may fragment to protect the core self. This is not a flaw but rather a sacred survival mechanism, an energetic dissociation that allows the individual to endure what might otherwise be unbearable. However, when these soul fragments remain unretrieved, they can leave a person feeling incomplete, numb, disconnected, or lost. One may notice repeating patterns of emotional pain, self-sabotage, or chronic fatigue that have no logical explanation. Spiritually, trauma can dim one's inner light, cloud one's sense of purpose, and distance one from the divine essence that once flowed freely. Healing the soul from trauma requires more than time; it asks for conscious reintegration, love, and the courageous act of calling home the parts of ourselves we had to leave behind. We restore wholeness and a profound sense of peace, clarity, and inner power through gentle therapeutic practices such as regression, soul retrieval, and energy healing. What deeply affects one person may not impact another in the same way. Each soul interprets and responds to life events through its lens of sensitivity, history, and perception. There is no universal measure for what constitutes trauma. It is defined by how it is felt and carried within. Let us now gently explore the various forms that trauma can take, honouring each one as valid and worthy of understanding.

Childhood trauma (abuse, neglect, abandonment).

The most profound soul loss often occurs in childhood, as this is when we are most vulnerable, impressionable, and dependent on others for safety and love. When a child experiences abuse, neglect, or abandonment, their developing psyche may dissociate or suppress painful memories as a survival mechanism. In an attempt to shield themselves from overwhelming fear, shame, or emotional pain, parts of their soul may fragment, retreating to a safe, hidden space in the subconscious. This loss can manifest in adulthood as low self-worth, difficulty forming secure relationships, chronic anxiety, or a deep-seated fear of rejection. Many individuals struggle to understand why they feel emotionally disconnected or unable to trust, not realising that aspects of their inner child remain frozen in past trauma. Healing requires inner child work, self-reparenting, and soul retrieval practices to gently reclaim these lost pieces, offering them the love, safety, and validation they never received. Through compassion, therapy, and spiritual healing, one can rewrite one's narrative, reintegrate one's fragmented self, and step into wholeness with newfound strength and self-acceptance. Abuse comes in many guises.

- **Abuse (physical, emotional, or sexual)** – If a child experiences repeated abuse, they may subconsciously detach from their body to escape the pain. This disconnection can follow them into adulthood, leading to difficulty trusting others, low self-worth, and emotional detachment.
- **Neglect** – A lack of emotional nurturing and validation can cause a child to feel unseen, unheard, or unworthy, leading to attachment issues and a chronic fear of rejection later in life.
- **Abandonment** – If a child is abandoned by a caregiver, either physically (through death, divorce, or absence) or emotionally (through neglect or disinterest), they may develop a fear of abandonment, co-dependency, or extreme independence as a protective mechanism.

How it manifests in adulthood:

Feeling emotionally numb or disconnected from memories of childhood.

Struggling to form deep, healthy relationships.

Fear of vulnerability, rejection, or abandonment.

Chronic feelings of unworthiness or needing to prove oneself.

This can be explored further in the Reconnecting with Your Inner Child Workbook.

Loss of a loved one (grief, unresolved emotions).

The sudden loss of a loved one can cause deep emotional trauma, leading to soul fragmentation if the grief is too overwhelming to process. In moments of profound loss, a person may feel like a piece of their soul has left with the departed, especially if they cannot mourn, find closure, or say goodbye correctly. This can create a lingering, energetic void where unresolved emotions such as guilt, regret, or longing keep the soul tethered to the past. Some may experience a sense of emptiness, numbness, or an inability to fully engage with life, as part of their energy remains in sorrow. Healing requires conscious grief work, soul retrieval, and spiritual practices that allow the bereaved to honour their loss while reclaiming the lost aspects of themselves. Through rituals, guided meditations, and connecting with the spirit of the departed healthily, one can find peace, restore their energetic wholeness, and move forward with love rather than pain.

How it manifests in adulthood:

Unresolved grief, depression, or a feeling of unfinished business.

Feeling like part of yourself is missing or life has lost meaning.

Experiencing repetitive dreams or visitations from the departed.

Difficulty forming new emotional bonds out of fear of loss.

Physical or emotional abuse.

When someone experiences ongoing physical or emotional abuse, their energy field becomes weakened, fragmented, and vulnerable, often leading to soul loss and deep emotional wounds. The repetitive nature of abuse, whether through violence, manipulation, gaslighting, or control, creates an environment of fear, helplessness, and emotional suppression. To survive, individuals may disconnect from their emotions, dissociate from their bodies, or suppress painful memories, unintentionally severing parts of their souls in the process. Over time, this can manifest as low self-worth, chronic anxiety, trust issues, or difficulty forming healthy relationships. Healing from abuse requires reclaiming lost soul fragments, restoring energetic boundaries, and rebuilding a sense of personal empowerment. Through inner child work, trauma-informed therapy, and energetic healing practices such as Reiki or soul retrieval, individuals can begin to release the grip of the past, rebuild self-trust, and reclaim their right to feel safe, whole, and loved. This applies to:

- Verbal and Emotional Abuse – Constant criticism, belittling, or manipulation can erode a person's sense of self-worth and identity, causing them to disconnect from their truth.
- Narcissistic Abuse – Being raised or being in a relationship with a narcissist can create extreme self-doubt, anxiety, and emotional detachment, making it feel like one's essence has been drained.

Definition of Gaslighting

Gaslighting is a form of emotional and psychological manipulation where a person intentionally makes someone doubt their perception, memory, or sanity. It often involves denying facts, minimising feelings, or twisting reality to gain control or power over another.

Definition of Narcissism

Narcissism refers to a personality trait or pattern of behaviour marked by excessive self-focus, a lack of empathy, and a strong need for admiration or validation. At its core, it often masks deep insecurity and emotional wounding.

How it manifests in adulthood:

Feeling powerless, voiceless, or trapped in survival mode.

Struggling with assertiveness and self-expression.

Fear of authority or confrontation.

Chronic low self-esteem and self-doubt.

Accidents or injuries that shock the system.

A sudden accident, injury, or medical emergency can cause a shock-induced soul fragmentation, where the mind and body experience an instantaneous split between physical reality and the energetic self. In moments of extreme pain, panic, or fear of death, the soul may partially detach as a survival mechanism, leading to energetic dissociation. This can result in lingering feelings of numbness, detachment, or an inability to fully process the trauma, even long after the physical wounds have healed. Some individuals may develop unexplained anxieties, phobias, or chronic pain as parts of their consciousness remain frozen in the moment of impact. Soul retrieval, energetic healing, and body-focused therapies such as somatic healing, Reiki, or breathwork can help reintegrate these lost aspects, allowing one to reconnect with their body, release residual fear, and reclaim their sense of wholeness and vitality.

- **Car Accidents or Falls** – Some people report out-of-body experiences or feeling detached after a traumatic physical event.
- **Surgical Trauma** – Some individuals feel like they "left part of themselves on the operating table" after significant surgery.
- **Near-Death Experiences (NDEs)** – Those who have been close to death may feel like a part of them never fully returned.

How it manifests in adulthood:

Feeling disconnected from the body.

Fear of hospitals, medical settings, or reminders of the trauma.

Chronic fatigue, weakness, or energy depletion.

Unexplained panic attacks or anxiety about safety.

Significant life changes (divorce, relocation, career shifts).

Significant life transitions can trigger soul loss, particularly when they involve sudden, forced, or emotionally turbulent changes that leave a person feeling uprooted, lost, or stripped of identity. Divorce, relocation, or career shifts can disrupt one's sense of stability, creating feelings of grief, uncertainty, and disconnection from one's purpose. These experiences may dismantle long-held beliefs, challenge personal security, and shake the foundations of self-worth, leading to a profound inner void. When a significant life change is accompanied by emotional trauma such as betrayal, financial hardship, or a loss of community, it can result in energetic fragmentation, where parts of the self remain trapped in the pain of the past. Healing requires reclaiming lost aspects of the soul, integrating transition lessons, and stepping forward with renewed clarity and empowerment. Through grounding practices, self-reflection, and conscious reinvention, one can restore a sense of belonging and purpose, embracing change as an opportunity for spiritual evolution rather than a loss of self.

- Divorce or Breakup – Ending a long-term relationship can feel like a piece of your soul was left with the other person.
- Relocation - Moving to a new city or country can cause a sense of disconnection from one's roots, culture, and familiar energy.
- Losing a Job or Career Identity - If someone strongly identifies with their job, losing it can create a deep existential crisis and soul fragmentation.

How it manifests in adulthood:

Feeling like you don't belong or are "floating" in life.

Struggling with identity or purpose after a significant transition.

A sense of nostalgia, longing, or homesickness.

Difficulty trusting oneself or adapting to change.

Toxic relationships or energetic entanglements.

Emotionally, mentally, or spiritually draining relationships can lead to energetic siphoning and soul fragmentation, leaving individuals feeling exhausted, unbalanced, and disconnected from their true selves. These relationships, whether romantic, familial, or platonic, often involve manipulation, control, co-dependency, or emotional neglect, creating an unhealthy exchange of energy. In many cases, individuals may feel trapped, unable to break free due to deep-seated patterns of guilt, fear, or attachment wounds. Over time, these entanglements can deplete personal power, cloud intuition, and disrupt emotional well-being, making it difficult to set healthy boundaries or trust oneself. Healing from toxic relationships requires recognising the energetic imbalance, severing unhealthy cords, reclaiming lost fragments of the soul, and realigning with self-worth and sovereignty. Through conscious detachment, energetic cleansing, and inner work, one can restore one's sense of wholeness and attract relationships that nourish rather than drain.

- Toxic Family Relationships - Being surrounded by judgment, criticism, or control can cause someone to detach from their true self to survive.
- Energetic Cords from Past Relationships - Sometimes, soul fragments remain attached to ex-partners or toxic individuals, making it difficult to move on and fully reclaim personal power.

How it manifests in adulthood:

Feeling stuck in old relationship patterns.

Sensing an energetic pull or attachment to someone from the past.

Struggling with people-pleasing or co-dependency.

Betrayal and heartbreak.

Betrayal from someone we deeply trust can shatter the foundation of our soul, leading to feelings of disillusionment, grief, and a loss of innocence. When trust is broken, whether through deception, abandonment, or unfulfilled promises, it can create a deep wound within the heart and spirit. This kind of pain often triggers feelings of unworthiness, fear of vulnerability, and an inability to trust others or even oneself. Over time, unresolved betrayal can manifest as emotional barriers, self-sabotage, or difficulty forming healthy connections. Healing from betrayal requires acknowledging the pain, reclaiming personal power, and restoring faith in oneself and the universe. Through forgiveness, not as an absolution of the betrayer but as a liberation of the self, one can release the emotional weight and open the heart to love and trust again.

- Romantic Betrayal – A cheating partner or broken trust can create deep wounds, leading to fear of intimacy and self-doubt.
- Friendship Betrayal – Feeling backstabbed or abandoned by a close friend can result in social withdrawal or isolation.
- Betrayal by Authority Figures – When a mentor, teacher, or leader betrays trust, it can create distrust in support systems.

How it manifests in adulthood:

Fear of trusting others or opening up emotionally.

Chronic relationship anxiety or self-sabotage.

Holding on to resentment or a need for revenge.

Suppression of emotions or forced conformity.

Being forced to suppress one's true self, emotions, or beliefs can lead to deep soul fragmentation. When individuals are conditioned to silence their authentic feelings, whether due to societal expectations, family dynamics, or cultural pressures, they disconnect from their inner truth. This suppression can manifest as anxiety, depression, emotional numbness, or a persistent sense of emptiness. Forced conformity, whether in childhood or adulthood, teaches individuals to prioritise external approval over their emotional well-being, leading to a loss of identity and inner conflict. Over time, this emotional repression can create energetic blockages, resulting in difficulty expressing emotions, setting boundaries, or fully stepping into one's power. Healing this wound requires reconnecting with the suppressed parts of oneself, embracing self-expression, and allowing repressed emotions to surface in a safe and supportive way.

- Strict Upbringing—Growing up in a household where emotions are not allowed can cause one to disconnect from one's authentic self.
- Forced Religious or Cultural Beliefs – Suppressing one's own spiritual or sexual identity can lead to inner conflict and self-rejection.

How it manifests in adulthood:

Feeling emotionally repressed or afraid to be authentic.

Chronic people-pleasing and fear of judgment.

Repressed past life trauma.

Sometimes, soul loss does not originate in this lifetime but comes from unresolved trauma carried over from past lives. Repressed past life trauma occurs when unresolved pain, fears, or experiences from a previous incarnation carry over into the present lifetime, often manifesting as irrational fears, unexplained emotional triggers, or recurring dreams. These imprints may stem from past life events such as early death, persecution, betrayal, or abandonment, leaving an energetic residue that continues to influence one's current emotions, relationships, and life choices. Without conscious awareness, an individual may feel a deep sense of unresolved grief, anxiety, or resistance toward certain people, places, or situations. Healing repressed past life trauma through past life regression, soul retrieval, or energetic clearing can help to release old wounds, restore balance, and clarify one's soul's journey.

How it manifests in adulthood:

Irrational fears or phobias with no logical explanation.

Feeling profoundly connected or repelled by specific places or people.

Recurring dreams or memories of past lifetimes.

When a soul fragment separates from the soul, it often carries specific emotions, memories, or qualities of the person's essence. Because soul loss usually occurs as a survival response, it is not necessarily harmful. However, leaving unhealed can lead to long-term emotional and spiritual imbalances.

This can result in symptoms such as:

Feeling incomplete or disconnected from oneself.

Chronic fatigue or lack of motivation.

Depression or emotional numbness.

Struggles with self-worth and confidence.

A persistent sense of longing or emptiness.

Feeling like you're "not all here" or "stuck".

Difficulty forming deep, authentic relationships.

Your soul has a history older than time. You have walked many roads, lived many lives, and each experience has shaped the wisdom you carry within.

Dr. Brian Weiss

The Process of Soul Retrieval

How Soul Retrieval works.

Soul retrieval is a sacred healing practice designed to reclaim lost aspects of the self that have fragmented due to trauma, grief, or significant life events. It is typically facilitated by a shamanic practitioner, energy healer, or hypnotherapist, who guides the individual into a deep, altered state of consciousness through hypnosis, guided meditation, rhythmic drumming, or breathwork. This altered state allows the individual to access the subconscious mind, spiritual planes, or the Akashic records, where lost soul fragments may reside. The practitioner or the individual will journey through symbolic landscapes, ancestral connections, or past life imprints to locate these missing pieces. Once found, the practitioner gently facilitates the reintegration of these soul fragments into the person's energy field, often through visualisation, breathwork, or ritual practices. This profoundly personal process can bring emotional release, newfound clarity, and renewed inner peace. After a soul retrieval session, individuals may experience a gradual reawakening of lost memories, emotional resilience, and a stronger connection to their authentic selves. To support full reintegration, grounding techniques, self-care practices, and ongoing reflection are essential, helping the person to embody their restored wholeness and move forward with renewed vitality.

Preparation and intention setting.

- The practitioner and client discuss the issues at hand, exploring symptoms of soul loss and identifying patterns that may indicate when and why the fragmentation occurred.
- The client sets a clear intention for healing, focusing on areas of life where they seek restoration and empowerment.

Entering a trance or journeying state.

- The practitioner may use drumming, breathwork, visualisation, guided meditation, or hypnosis to help the client enter a deep, relaxed state.
- Some practitioners work in altered states of consciousness (shamanic journeying), while others guide the client through self-discovery and inner exploration.

Locating the lost soul fragments.

- The practitioner, often with the assistance of spirit guides, power animals, or higher beings, searches the spiritual realm for the missing pieces of the person's soul.
- These fragments may be found in specific memories, past life experiences, or energetic realms, appearing as a younger version of the client, an object, or an energy form.

Communicating with the soul fragment.

- The practitioner (or client) engages with the lost fragment, asking it why it left, what it needs to return, and how it can be healed.
- Sometimes, the soul fragment may hold fear, pain, or grief and require reassurance and healing before reintegration.

Healing and reintegration.

- The soul fragment is gently brought back into the client's energy field, heart space, or third eye, often accompanied by a healing ritual, light activation, or breathwork.
- The client may feel an immediate sense of warmth, emotional release, or deep inner peace.

Grounding and Integration.

- After the session, the client is guided through grounding exercises to integrate the returned energy fully.
- Journaling, meditation, self-care, and affirmations are recommended to help the soul fragment reintegrate fully into daily life.

Effects of Soul Retrieval.

Soul retrieval can bring profound healing and transformation. Some people experience immediate shifts, while others notice gradual changes as the soul fragment fully reintegrates. Some benefits include:

- A renewed sense of self and purpose.
- Emotional healing from past wounds.
- Increased energy, motivation, and joy.
- Deepened spiritual awareness and intuition.
- Greater self-love and acceptance.
- Healing of old relationship patterns.
- A stronger connection to the inner child.

How to support soul integration after a retrieval.

Once a soul fragment has been returned, nurturing and integrating it into your life is essential. Here are some key ways to support the process:

Journaling: Write about any emotions, memories, or insights that arise after your session.
After a past life regression or healing session, journaling can be a powerful tool to integrate your experiences and gain more profound clarity. Writing allows you to explore any emotions, memories, or insights that surface during your journey without judgment or restriction. Pay attention to recurring patterns, sensations, or feelings, as these may hold valuable messages from your subconscious. Did any particular period, setting, or relationship stand out? Were there emotions that felt unusually strong or familiar? Perhaps you gained a new perspective on a current challenge or uncovered a soul lesson carried across lifetimes. By capturing these thoughts in your journal, you create a sacred record of your healing journey, allowing you to reflect, connect the dots, and revisit your insights as your understanding deepens. If certain emotions feel unresolved, you may also use your journal to write letters to your past self, spirit guides, or even to a past life version, offering compassion, wisdom, and closure.

Meditation and Reflection: Connect with your reclaimed energy.
After a soul retrieval or past life healing session, meditation and quiet reflection are essential for integrating the energy that has returned to you. Find a peaceful space to sit or lie down undisturbed, allowing yourself to focus on your breath gently. As you breathe deeply, visualise the reclaimed energy flowing back into your body, filling any spaces that once felt empty or disconnected. Notice any sensations, emotions, or inner messages that arise. Does this energy feel familiar, comforting, or even transformative? Take a moment to express gratitude for this reconnection, honouring the journey that led you here. If your mind wanders, gently bring it back by placing a hand over your heart or solar plexus, affirming, "I welcome back all parts of my soul with love and wholeness." Reflection after meditation can offer more profound clarity, helping you understand how this healing experience may influence your emotions, thoughts, or even how you move forward. Journaling any insights that arise can further solidify this reconnection, ensuring that your reclaimed energy becomes a fully integrated and empowered part of you.

Self-Love Practices: Engage in activities that make you feel safe, joyful, and whole.
True healing begins with self-love, and engaging in nurturing activities helps to reinforce feelings of safety, joy, and wholeness after past life healing or soul retrieval. Choose deeply comforting practices such as spending time in nature, creating art, dancing freely, journaling, or simply resting without guilt. Please consider what brings you inner peace and fully allow yourself to experience it. Self-love also includes setting healthy boundaries, speaking kindly to yourself, and honouring your emotions without judgment. You may wish to create daily rituals that ground and centre you, such as placing a hand over your heart and affirming, "I am whole, I am safe, I am loved." Acts of self-care, whether a warm bath, mindful breathing, or surrounding yourself with uplifting music, reinforce the message that you are worthy of love from others and yourself. The more you prioritise joyful and healing activities, the stronger your connection to your inner self becomes, helping you step forward with renewed energy and soul alignment.

Expression: Art, music, movement, and storytelling help ground the soul's energy.
Creativity is a powerful bridge between the conscious and subconscious mind, allowing the soul's energy to ground and integrate after deep healing work. Art, music, movement, and storytelling provide a sacred outlet for flowing emotions, memories, and newfound awareness. Painting, drawing, or sculpting can visually translate inner experiences, offering insight into past lives or soul fragments that have returned. Music, whether listening, singing, or playing an instrument, vibrationally aligns the soul with its authentic frequency, helping to release stored emotions and encourage self-expression. Movement, such as dance, yoga, or intuitive body flow, allows the body to release stagnant energy while embodying the lightness and renewal of healing. Whether written or spoken, storytelling brings voice to the soul's journey, turning lessons into wisdom and experiences into personal transformation. Engaging in creative expression is not about perfection but about allowing the soul's essence to manifest in tangible form, strengthening the connection between past, present, and future.

Affirmations: Repeat statements like "I am whole. I welcome back all parts of me."
Affirmations are powerful tools for soul integration and transformation, reinforcing the belief that healing is possible and that all lost or fragmented parts of the self can return home. By repeating affirmations such as "I am whole. I welcome back all parts of me," or "I am safe, I am loved, I am complete," you are reprogramming the subconscious mind and aligning your energy with the truth of your divine essence. Spoken aloud, written in a journal, or whispered in moments of stillness, these affirmations act as energetic commands, calling back the soul's vitality and restoring balance. The key is to feel the words as you say them to let them vibrate through your body and spirit, dissolving old fears and reinforcing the reality of your healing. Integrating these sacred statements into your daily practice, you embody the energy of wholeness, allowing each affirmation to weave a new, empowered narrative for your life.

Boundaries: Do not re-engage with situations or people contributing to the soul loss.

Healthy boundaries are vital to soul retrieval, ensuring your reclaimed energy remains protected and nurtured. When we re-engage with situations, relationships, or environments that initially contributed to our soul loss, we risk repeating old patterns of depletion, disempowerment, and emotional wounding. Establishing firm yet compassionate boundaries allows you to honour your healing, safeguarding the newfound wholeness and strength you have cultivated. This may involve limiting contact with toxic individuals, saying no to commitments that drain your spirit, or creating physical and energetic space for your continued growth. Boundaries are not about rejection; they are about self-respect and preservation. As you strengthen your inner sovereignty, remind yourself: "I have the right to protect my energy. I choose relationships and experiences that nourish my soul." In doing so, you create a sacred container for your healing, allowing your reclaimed energy to flourish in alignment with your highest self.

The connection between Soul Retrieval and Past Lives.

Soul loss can sometimes originate in past lives, where unresolved trauma causes fragments of the soul to remain attached to another time or dimension. Past life regression and soul retrieval work beautifully together in these cases, helping individuals reclaim lost aspects of their essence from other incarnations. For example, someone struggling with unexplained fears or karmic cycles may find that a soul fragment remains stuck in a past lifetime where they experienced deep trauma or betrayal. By retrieving this piece and healing its wounds, they can finally break free from limiting patterns and step into a new level of personal empowerment. This process is often deeply transformational, bringing healing to the present and creating harmony across the soul's entire timeline. When a lost soul fragment is retrieved from a past life, the individual often experiences a profound sense of wholeness, clarity, and inner peace. Emotional burdens that once felt unexplainable begin to lift, and behaviours that seemed fixed or habitual may suddenly shift. This reunion of soul parts restores vitality and reawakens inner wisdom that has long been forgotten. It is a homecoming where the fragmented self is welcomed back with compassion, understanding, and spiritual grace. In doing so, the soul is no longer fractured by time but unified in its divine expression across lifetimes.

Final thoughts.

Soul retrieval is a powerful and sacred process that helps individuals reconnect with their true essence, personal power, and spiritual wholeness. It allows for deep emotional and energetic healing, assisting people to move forward with greater clarity, strength, and self-awareness. By reclaiming all parts of yourself, you step into a more authentic and empowered version of who you were always meant to be.

The past and future are illusions. The soul exists in the eternal now, carrying wisdom from lifetime to lifetime.

Edgar Cayce

Affirmations

Restore Your Power & Energy

Affirmations

When a soul has experienced trauma, fragmentation, or prolonged emotional pain, it often results in a depletion of personal power and life force energy. This can manifest as chronic fatigue, emotional numbness, lack of motivation, or an ongoing feeling of being stuck. Restoring your energy is not just about feeling better. It's about reawakening your divine essence, reclaiming your sacred autonomy, and reconnecting with the radiant soul spark that animates your life. Rituals and affirmations are potent tools for soul restoration. Through simple yet intentional practices, we can energetically call back parts of ourselves that have been scattered, silenced, or suppressed. These practices serve as sacred containers for healing, using intention, vibration, and spiritual will to invite wholeness. Affirmations serve as healing declarations and soul reminders, spoken aloud or written down, that reshape inner belief systems and realign the subconscious with love, strength, and purpose.

How to Write a Soul Affirmation.

A soul affirmation is a sacred declaration that aligns your thoughts and energy with the truth of your highest self. When writing a soul affirmation, begin by tuning into your heart. What is it that your soul longs to believe, embody, or heal? Use present-tense language, starting with "I am," "I trust," or "I welcome." Keep the phrasing clear, positive, and emotionally resonant. Avoid negatives (such as "don't" or "won't") and instead affirm what is true for you, even if it's something you are still growing into. A powerful soul affirmation might sound like: "I am whole, I am safe, and I return to myself with love." Speak it, write it, and feel it repeating your affirmation daily, which helps to anchor its truth deep within your spirit. These affirmations can be spoken during meditation, written in a journal, whispered into your heart each morning, or integrated into ritual work. Affirmations become even more potent when paired with embodiment when you say the words and begin to live them. You are not just speaking to your conscious mind each time you affirm your truth. You talk directly to the wounded parts of your soul that long to be seen, held, and believed in. These words become soul nourishment, gently reprogramming limiting beliefs and outdated patterns. Over time, affirmations help shift the energy field around you, acting as a magnetic force that calls for healing, alignment, and grace. As you consistently return to your affirmations with reverence and intention, you build a new spiritual architecture within a safe inner temple where your spirit can rest, rise, and radiate. Trust that even if the change feels subtle, every word spoken in love echoes throughout your energy field, awakening the deep remembrance of who you indeed are.

We are not human beings having a spiritual experience. We are spiritual beings having a human experience.

Pierre Teilhard de Chardin

Examples of Soul Affirmations

I reclaim all parts of my power with love and grace.

I am safe to be fully present in my body and life.

I am whole; I am radiant; I am sovereign.

I call back my energy from all times, all places, and all dimensions.

I am whole, and all parts of me are welcome here.

I am safe to remember, to release, and to heal.

I return to myself with love, patience, and grace.

I honour the wisdom of my soul's journey across lifetimes.

I trust that all I need is already within me.

I am supported, guided, and protected by divine forces.

I allow my light to shine without fear or apology.

I release what no longer serves my highest good.

I am deeply connected to my intuition and inner knowing.

I choose love, truth, and freedom in every moment.

I am grounded, present, and aligned with my soul's path.

My energy is sacred, and I honour it with care.

I forgive myself and others, and I choose peace.

I embrace my past, learn from it, and release it with love.

I walk forward with confidence, clarity, and trust in the universe.

I reclaim my power and return to my divine essence.

My voice matters, my story matters, and my healing matters.

I invite joy, creativity, and magic into my life.

I belong here. I am worthy. I am enough.

Take some time now to write affirmations that will support your soul as it is now.

Akashic Records

A Gateway to the Soul's Infinite Wisdom

The Akashic Records are believed to be a vast, energetic library containing the collective knowledge, experiences, and imprints of every soul. This mystical archive holds every thought, action, emotion, and intention that has ever been expressed in any lifetime past, present, or even potential future reality. Sometimes referred to as the "Book of Life" or the "Cosmic Mind," the Akashic Records are an interdimensional source of wisdom and spiritual insight, accessible to those who seek guidance for soul growth, healing, and evolution. In spiritual traditions, the term "Akasha" is derived from Sanskrit, meaning "ether" or "sky," signifying the non-physical realm where these records are stored. This energetic field is said to exist beyond time and space, acting as a universal consciousness that connects every soul to divine knowledge. Some describe it as a quantum database of all existence, where information is imprinted in subtle energy patterns that can be accessed through deep meditation, hypnosis, dreams, or guided spiritual practices.

What Are the Akashic Records?

The Akashic Records are a spiritual repository of every thought, action, and experience your soul has had. Learning to access them can clarify recurring patterns, karmic lessons, and unresolved past life issues.

What can be found in the Akashic Records?

The Akashic Records contain limitless wisdom and information about an individual's past lives, present experiences, karmic lessons, soul contracts, and future possibilities. The records store:

1. **Personal soul history** – Your past lives, relationships, soul connections, and significant life events.
2. **Karmic patterns and lessons** – Insights into challenges you repeatedly face and how to heal them.
3. **Soul contracts and life purpose** – Agreements made before birth with people, places, and events to shape your growth.
4. **Spiritual gifts and talents** – Abilities you have mastered in past incarnations that can be reawakened.
5. **Healing unresolved trauma** – Guidance on releasing deep-seated fears, emotional wounds, and limiting beliefs.
6. **Potential future pathways** – Probable outcomes based on current energies, allowing you to shift timelines consciously.

Each soul has its own "book" or "record", and it is believed that spirit guides, masters, and beings of light guard these sacred archives. This divine knowledge can provide profound healing, clarity, and purpose in one's present incarnation.

How do the Akashic Records work?

The Akashic Records operate like an interdimensional memory field, recording every soul's journey across multiple lifetimes. Some spiritual traditions compare them to an energetic imprint of the universe, much like a giant database that stores the cause and effect of every thought, word, and deed. Since these records exist outside of linear time, they do not "predict" the future in a fixed way. Instead, they reveal potential timelines based on the trajectory of one's current choices. This means that free will plays a crucial role in one's destiny. Some believe that highly intuitive individuals, psychics, and energy healers naturally access the Akashic Records through deep meditative states, hypnosis, or altered consciousness. Certain practices, such as prayer, sacred rituals, and guided visualisation, can also serve as portals to retrieve information from this cosmic archive.

How to access the Akashic Records.

While some individuals naturally enter the Akashic field in dreams, meditations, or deep spiritual work, others can develop the ability through structured techniques. Here's a simple process:

1. **Prepare Your Space** – Sit in a quiet, undisturbed place with a journal to record your insights.
2. **Set an Intention** – Formulate a specific question or topic (e.g., *What karmic lessons am I currently working through?*).
3. **Enter a Meditative State** – Close your eyes, focus on your breath, and visualise yourself walking into a vast, celestial library.
4. **Meet the Guardians** – Imagine encountering a spiritual guide, record keeper, or light being who grants access to your soul's book.
5. **Open Your Record** – See a golden book or scroll with your name. Allow messages, symbols, or memories to surface.
6. **Write Down What You Receive** – Keep a journal to track the imagery, emotions, or insights that arise.
7. **Express Gratitude** – Before closing the session, thank the guides and guardians.

Each lifetime is a piece of the greater story your soul is trying to tell.

Elena Brower

Why access the Akashic Records?

Exploring the Akashic Records can lead to profound transformation by helping individuals:

Understand patterns and struggles – Recognize recurring cycles and how to break them.

The Akashic Records serve as a spiritual blueprint, containing the vast accumulation of every thought, action, and experience your soul has encountered across lifetimes. When exploring these records, one of the most profound revelations is recognising recurring life patterns and struggle themes repeated across multiple incarnations, shaping your present reality. These patterns may manifest as relationship dynamics, fears, karmic debts, limiting beliefs, or persistent obstacles that seem to follow you despite your best efforts to change. By accessing the Akashic field, you gain a broader perspective, allowing you to trace the origins of these cycles and understand their more profound purpose. The key to breaking these patterns lies in awareness and conscious transformation, identifying the lesson or soul contract within the repetition, healing unresolved wounds, and making new, empowered choices that align with your highest path. The Akashic Records act as a mirror, showing you the energetic threads woven through your lifetimes and offering insights into how to rewrite your narrative, liberate yourself from stagnation, and step into soul-aligned growth and freedom.

Heal past life wounds – Releasing trauma carried over from previous incarnations.

The Akashic Records hold the energetic imprint of all your past incarnations, including the unresolved wounds and traumas that may still affect you in this lifetime. Many emotional struggles, fears, and even physical ailments stem from karmic imprints carried forward from previous lifetimes. These wounds can manifest as phobias with no logical origin, recurring relationship challenges, patterns of self-sabotage, or deep-seated fears that seem unexplainable. By accessing the Akashic field, you can uncover the root cause of these energetic blockages and begin the release, healing, and integration process. Acknowledging and understanding the source of pain allows you to work through it on a soul level, freeing yourself from the emotional and spiritual burdens that have carried over across lifetimes. You can reclaim lost energy, resolve unfinished lessons, and cut energetic cords that no longer serve your highest good through guided meditation, Akashic inquiry, or regression therapy. Healing past life wounds through the Akashic Records is a profoundly liberating process, allowing you to step into this lifetime with renewed clarity, purpose, and emotional freedom, fully empowered to live without the weight of the past holding you back.

Awaken spiritual gifts – Rediscover abilities mastered in past lifetimes.

The Akashic Records hold the blueprint of your soul's journey across lifetimes, including the spiritual gifts, talents, and wisdom you have cultivated over many incarnations. Many individuals feel drawn to certain mystical practices, healing modalities, or creative pursuits without prior training. In this lifetime, these innate abilities often stem from past life mastery. By accessing the Akashic field, you can uncover the skills and knowledge that your soul has already developed, allowing you to reactivate dormant gifts such as energy healing, divination, clairvoyance, mediumship, herbalism, sacred rituals, or even ancient wisdom traditions. Often, these talents may feel familiar or intuitive, as if you are remembering rather than learning. Exploring your soul's history within the Akashic Records can help you reconnect with these latent abilities, integrate them into your spiritual practice, and use them for personal growth or service to others. When you awaken the spiritual gifts from past lifetimes, you reclaim the wisdom and power of your eternal soul, aligning more deeply with your true purpose in this incarnation.

Strengthen relationships – Understand soul contracts and karmic ties with others.

The Akashic Records offer profound insight into the soul contracts and karmic relations that shape our relationships. Every significant connection- family, friends, lovers, or even adversaries- has a deeper spiritual purpose. These relationships often extend across multiple lifetimes, with souls coming together to teach, heal, challenge, or support one another in their spiritual evolution. By accessing the Akashic Records, you can uncover the karmic lessons behind your relationships, gaining clarity on recurring patterns, unresolved conflicts, or deep-seated emotional bonds. Understanding these connections allows you to release old wounds, forgive past transgressions, and approach relationships with greater compassion and awareness. Whether you seek closure, healing, or a stronger connection with a loved one, the Akashic Records help illuminate the higher purpose of your relationships, guiding you toward greater harmony, balance, and soul-aligned connections in this lifetime.

Align with your highest purpose – Gain clarity on your soul's path for this lifetime.

The Akashic Records serve as a divine blueprint of your soul's journey, holding the wisdom of your past, present, and future potential. By accessing these records, you can gain profound clarity on your soul's purpose, the lessons you came here to learn, the gifts you are meant to share, and the path that will bring you the greatest fulfillment. Life's challenges and distractions can often cloud our vision, making it difficult to see the deeper meaning behind our experiences. The Akashic Records help you reconnect with your soul's mission, revealing the passions, talents, and spiritual callings that align with your highest self. Whether you seek guidance on career, relationships, or personal growth, the records provide insight into how you can best serve the world while staying true to your authentic essence. Aligning with your soul's purpose allows you to live with intention, embrace your divine potential, and walk your path confidently and spiritually.

Many find that accessing the Akashic Records provides validation, wisdom, and peace, offering a higher perspective beyond ego or immediate earthly concerns.

Final thoughts.

The Akashic Records are not just about retrieving information—they are a portal to self-realisation and enlightenment. When approached with an open heart and pure intention, they offer deep healing, clarity, and empowerment, guiding souls toward their highest evolution.

Guided Akashic Records Meditation Script

A journey to access your soul's wisdom.

Preparation.

Before beginning, choose how you wish to engage with this meditation. You may read through the entire script first to familiarise yourself with the journey and then return to it in quiet contemplation. Alternatively, you may move through the script more interactively, pausing after each section to reflect and record your impressions, insights, or answers as if completing a sacred soul assignment. Both approaches are powerful, so trust your intuition to guide you to what feels right for you now.

To start, find a quiet, comfortable place where you won't be disturbed. Sit or lie down, close your eyes, and take a few deep, cleansing breaths. Let your body relax completely.

Opening invocation.

"I call upon my highest self, my spirit guides, and the guardians of the Akashic Records. I ask to be surrounded by divine light, love, and protection as I enter this sacred space. May only truth, wisdom, and guidance for my highest good be revealed now. So, it is."

Deep relaxation and grounding.

Take a deep breath in and slowly exhale. With each breath, allow your body to relax even more. Feel yourself sinking deeper into a sense of peace and stillness. With your next breath, imagine golden light streaming down from above, flowing into the crown of your head, filling you with warmth and divine energy. Imagine this light flowing through your body, relaxing your shoulders and softening your chest, moving down through your arms, hands, and fingertips, flowing through your spine, hips, legs, and feet and grounding you deeply into the Earth. With each breath, you feel lighter, more expansive, yet deeply connected to all that is.

The sacred library entrance.

Now, in your mind's eye, envision yourself standing before a magnificent ancient library. Its golden doors shimmer with energy, radiating wisdom, welcoming you in. Notice the intricate carvings on the doors, symbols, runes, or sacred geometry unique to you. This is the entrance to your Akashic Records. As you step forward, a gentle presence greets you, a guardian of the records. They bow slightly, acknowledging your arrival. They invite you to state your full name aloud or in your mind.

(Pause here to allow yourself to say your name.)

The guardian nods, recognising you, and with a sweep of their hand, the doors begin to open.

Entering the Akashic Records.

You step inside and find yourself in a vast, luminous hall stretching endlessly in every direction. Rows upon rows of books, scrolls, and shimmering records float in the air, glowing with an ethereal light. The energy here feels deeply familiar, as if you have been here before because you have your guide gesturing toward a grand table, where a large, golden book awaits. This is your soul record, the book of your journey through time. With reverence, you touch the book, feel its energy, and sense the immense wisdom in its pages. As you take a deep breath, the book begins to open.

Receiving divine guidance.

Your eyes scan the pages, and images, words, or feelings begin to arise. Perhaps you see a past life. You may receive insight into a repeating pattern in your current life. Maybe a guide steps forward to share a message with you.

(Pause for 1-2 minutes to allow deep reflection.)

If you have a specific question, gently ask:

What wisdom do the Akashic Records wish to share with me today?

Observe what comes forward—whether through a vision, a sensation, or an intuitive knowing. Trust that the answers you need are being revealed at the perfect time.

(Pause for 1-2 minutes for deeper exploration.)

Expressing gratitude and closing the records.

Now, gently close the book, knowing you can return whenever you seek guidance. The guardian steps forward again, placing a hand on your shoulder in blessing. You express gratitude for the wisdom and divine insight you have received and the clarity that will unfold in the days ahead. As you turn to leave, the grand doors of the library slowly close behind you, sealing the sacred knowledge within a safe and waiting for your return.

You can also access this script as a recording on my YouTube Channel under the Workbook Tab. The details are at the back of the book.

Returning to the present.

Now, bring your awareness back to your breath. Feel your body, your hands, your feet, your surroundings. Take a deep breath in and exhale fully. Slowly wiggle your fingers and toes, bringing movement back into your body. When you are ready, gently open your eyes, feeling refreshed, clear, and deeply connected to your soul's wisdom.

Integration and reflection.

Take a moment to write down any insights, messages, or feelings that arose during your journey. Trust that the wisdom will unfold in divine timing, even if nothing seems clear. The Akashic Records are always available to you. The more you visit, the stronger your connection will become.

Final Reflection.

After journaling over the following pages, take a moment to re-read your insights. Trust that even if everything isn't immediately apparent, the wisdom you accessed will unfold in divine timing. The answers you seek are sometimes already within you, and the records help you remember.

Each lifetime is a chapter in the book of your soul. The lessons learned are never lost, only carried forward into the next adventure.

Deepak Chopra

Journal pages.

Journalling Prompts

Records Exploration

Use these prompts after your meditation to deepen your understanding and integrate the wisdom received from your journey into the Akashic Records.

1. Messages from the Records

What was the first sensation, image, or message you received upon entering the Akashic Records?

Did you see any symbols, numbers, or colours that stood out? What might they represent?

Did you receive specific guidance or wisdom about my soul's journey?

2. Exploring Past Lives

Did I experience a past life memory? If so, what period or location did it seem to be from?

What emotions surfaced while I explored my past life?

Is a pattern or lesson from this past life still affecting me?

3. Soul Contracts and Karmic Lessons

Did I sense any strong connections with certain people in my life?

What karmic lesson am I currently working through?

How can I shift my perspective or actions to heal this pattern?

4. Life Purpose and Spiritual Path

What insights did I receive about my soul's mission in this lifetime?

Did my records reveal any hidden gifts or abilities I must embrace?

What steps can I take today to align more fully with my highest path?

5. Healing and Growth

Did the records reveal any unresolved wounds or emotional blockages?

What message did my higher self or spirit guide share about healing?

What is the most critical shift I need to make in my life right now?

6. Future Pathways and Divine Timing

Did I glimpse any potential future paths for myself?

How do I feel about the future insights I received? Excited? Anxious? Inspired?

What actions can I take now to move toward my highest possible future?

7. Deepening my connection to the records.

How did I feel while accessing the Akashic Records?

What techniques helped me feel most connected?

How can I strengthen my ability to access the records more clearly in the future?

Soul Contracts

Understanding Soul Contracts

The sacred agreements of the soul.

A soul contract is a pre-incarnation agreement between souls before entering a new lifetime. These contracts outline the lessons, experiences, relationships, and karmic cycles a soul has undertaken to grow, evolve, and fulfill its spiritual purpose. These agreements are not forced upon us; they are created with our free will in collaboration with our higher self, spirit guides, and the divine. Soul contracts influence the people we meet, our challenges, and the opportunities that shape our journey. While they are designed for our growth, they can sometimes manifest as painful relationships, difficult circumstances, or repeating life patterns, pushing us toward greater awareness and healing. Understanding these contracts allows us to navigate life more clearly, making empowered choices that align with our highest path.

How soul contracts are formed.

Before we incarnate, our soul undergoes a planning process in the spiritual realm, often within the Akashic Records, where we review past lives and determine what we need to experience in the next incarnation. Some key elements of a soul contract include:

Life lessons – What themes or challenges will we need to work through? (e.g., self-love, forgiveness, trust, courage, independence).

Karmic balancing – Are there unresolved actions or energies from past lives that need to be healed or balanced?

Key relationships – Who will play significant roles in our journey? (e.g., family, friends, romantic partners, mentors, rivals).

Soul missions and purpose – What work will we do in this life to expand our soul and contribute to the world?

Divine timing and free will – While specific lessons and connections are prearranged, we always have the free will to respond differently and alter the course of our path.

Types of Soul Contracts

Soul contracts are highly unique to each individual, but there are common types that many experience:

1. **Karmic contracts.**

Karmic contracts arise from past-life debts, imbalances, or unresolved experiences that need healing. They often appear as challenging relationships or repetitive struggles that push us to break toxic cycles, forgive, and learn higher lessons. While these contracts can be painful, they ultimately guide us toward greater wisdom and growth.

2. **Soulmate and twin flame contracts.**

These contracts involve deep, spiritual relationships that help us expand in love, awareness, and personal transformation. Soulmates can be romantic partners, family members, or close friends, while twin flames mirror our soul's essence, often triggering profound personal growth. Depending on the lessons involved, these contracts can be harmonious or deeply challenging.

3. **Teacher-student contracts.**

These agreements involve mentors, spiritual guides, or influential figures who cross our paths to teach us something profound. These relationships may be temporary or lifelong, but they give us the wisdom and knowledge needed to evolve.

4. **Healer-wounded contracts.**

In these agreements, one soul is a healer or guide while the other experiences pain or struggles that require assistance. These contracts are standard in therapists, healers, caregivers, and spiritual leaders who may feel an innate calling to help others.

5. **Life-purpose contracts.**

These mission-driven contracts influence our careers, passions, and spiritual work. They align with our soul's higher purpose, guiding us toward specific callings or contributions that benefit humanity and the planet.

Breaking, releasing, and rewriting soul contracts.

While soul contracts are designed for growth, some may become outdated, limiting, or unnecessarily painful as we evolve. Fortunately, contracts can be reviewed, rewritten, or released when they no longer serve our highest good.

Signs a soul contract needs releasing.

You feel trapped in a repeating cycle with no resolution.

A relationship or situation drains your energy without growth.

You've learned the lesson, but the bond still feels restrictive.

You feel an intuitive calling to move on but struggle to do so.

Methods for Releasing Soul Contracts.

Meditation and Akashic Record Access – Enter a deep meditative state and ask your higher self or guides to reveal outdated contracts.

Ritual Burning Ceremony – Write down the contract you wish to release, thank it for its lessons, and burn it as a symbol of release.

Energetic Cord Cutting – Visualize severing any lingering energy ties with an individual or experience that no longer serves you.

Affirmation and Intention Setting – Reaffirm your new path with statements like:

"I release all outdated contracts that no longer serve my highest good."

"I am free from karmic ties that limit my growth."

Final Thoughts: Embracing the Power of Soul Contracts.

Soul contracts are potent tools of evolution that shape our experiences, relationships, and lessons in this lifetime. Whether they bring love, challenge, healing, or transformation, each contract is an opportunity for growth and soul expansion. By becoming aware of these agreements, we can navigate our journey with wisdom, consciously heal past patterns, and align with our highest potential. Above all, remember that you are the creator of your destiny. Soul contracts are written in collaboration with the divine, and you always have the power to rewrite your story and embrace your true soul's path. Working with a Regression Therapist or Energy Healer. A trained professional can help guide you through contract identification and clearing.

Identifying Soul Contracts – The agreements we make before incarnating.

Before birth, our souls create sacred agreements known as soul contracts, which outline the key relationships, experiences, and lessons we will encounter in this lifetime. These contracts are made in the spiritual realms before incarnation, with the guidance of higher beings such as spirit guides, ancestors, and our higher selves. Soul contracts are not about predestination but spiritual growth and karmic evolution. They serve as opportunities to heal past wounds, balance karma, and expand our consciousness. These agreements can manifest through relationships with family, friends, lovers, mentors, and even challenging individuals who push us to grow. Some contracts are based on love and support, while others involve difficult or painful lessons that encourage transformation. By exploring our Akashic Records or deep self-reflection, we can gain insight into these soul agreements, allowing us to navigate our relationships and experiences with greater awareness, acceptance, and wisdom. Recognising a soul contract helps us move from resistance to empowerment, understanding that every encounter, positive or challenging, is part of a greater divine plan.

Rewriting and releasing old contracts – Rituals to clear outdated soul agreements.

Some soul contracts may become outdated, restrictive, or misaligned with our highest path as we evolve spiritually. While these contracts were once essential for our growth, they can sometimes keep us stuck in repetitive patterns, unhealthy relationships, or karmic cycles that no longer serve us. Releasing or rewriting these agreements allows us to reclaim our spiritual sovereignty and move forward with greater clarity and freedom. One powerful way to release old contracts is through rituals and intentional energy work. A common practice is the soul contract burning ritual, where you write down the contract you wish to release, acknowledging the lesson it taught you, and then burn the paper as a symbol of transformation and closure. Another method is guided meditation, where you enter a deep state of relaxation, visualise the contract before you, and rewrite it with new intentions that align with your present soul growth. Calling upon your higher self, spirit guides, or Akashic Records can also provide insight into which contracts need releasing and how to create new agreements that support your evolution. By consciously clearing outdated soul contracts, you break free from energetic entanglements, dissolve lingering karmic imbalances, and step into a new chapter of life with greater empowerment, self-awareness, and spiritual alignment.

Reincarnation is not an idea to be believed in; it is a truth to be remembered.

Lama Surya Das

Exercise: Write a letter to your Akashic Records keeper, asking for insights on a recurring life pattern.

Are you aware of any of your soul contracts or themes that you are currently working on?

Spirit Guides & Helpers

Walking with Unseen Allies on Your Soul Journey

From the moment we are born and even before, we are accompanied by an invisible circle of light beings who walk beside us: our spirit guides and tribe of helpers. These beings exist in the spiritual realms and are dedicated to guiding, protecting, teaching, and supporting us throughout our life journey. While invisible to the naked eye, their presence can be felt through intuition, synchronicities, dreams, and deep inner knowing.

What Are Spirit Guides?

Spirit Guides are non-physical beings whose role is to support a soul's evolution across lifetimes, dimensions, and throughout time and space. There is ongoing debate about the true nature of a spirit guide's energy. Still, from my many years of experience facilitating Past Life Regression (PLR) and Life Between Lives (LBL) sessions, I have come to understand the following:

Your spirit guide is not, and has never been, biologically related to the soul they are guiding. Guides are specialised energies or entities who undergo dedicated training and mentoring to guide and assist a soul with its life themes in alignment with the soul's pre-birth contract.

Across the hundreds of sessions I've conducted, I have never encountered a spirit guide who was also a family member of the person being guided. This means that your beloved nana or a parent who passed during your early years is not your spirit guide. While they may still visit, support, or check in on you from the spirit world, they are not assigned to guide your soul through its incarnation. Sometimes, a guide may have shared a distant or ancient incarnation with the soul they are now guiding, but they are not members of the same primary soul group. In fact, I believe that guides are purposefully not part of your soul group, allowing them to offer objective, non-attached guidance rooted in your highest and greatest good.

That said, it is certainly possible to encounter passed-over loved ones during spiritual journeys or soul work. These souls may appear to offer love, reassurance, or comfort, but they are distinct from your guiding energies. Most people have a collective of spiritual helpers, a loving team that may include a primary or lifelong guide and temporary guides who step in for specific life chapters, challenges, or spiritual initiations. This guiding tribe can also include spirit animals, celestial beings, or even interdimensional and extraterrestrial energies. Each guide carries a unique frequency and function: some offer protection, while others bring healing, creative insight, emotional guidance, or spiritual teachings. They never override your free will but instead offer gentle nudges, inspiration, and signs as you move through life. These guides are with you from before birth and often remain through many incarnations. As with all spiritual teachings, it's essential to do your own research, tune into your intuition, and explore what resonates with you. Your beliefs about spirit guides are yours to shape, and trust your inner knowing.

Types of Guides and Helpers.

Your spiritual team may include a variety of beings, such as:

Guardian Spirit Guides.

Guardian Spirit Guides are your lifelong protectors, assigned before birth to walk beside you through every twist and turn of your incarnation. Unlike temporary guides who assist with specific lessons or life chapters, Guardian Guides remain constant, quietly overseeing your soul's journey unfolding. Their primary role is to help you stay aligned with your soul contract, offering protection, inner nudges, and spiritual insight when you veer from your intended path. Though often subtle in their presence, their devotion is unwavering, and their guidance is always rooted in your highest good. These guides act as spiritual guardians, holding the blueprint of your life theme and supporting you in embodying your true potential across lifetimes.

Teacher Guides.

Teacher Guides are wisdom keepers and spiritual mentors who illuminate the path of learning and self-discovery. They are often called upon during deep soul growth, offering insights into spiritual truths, life purpose, and the lessons your soul has chosen to explore in this lifetime. These guides help you understand the "why" behind your experiences, encouraging reflection, integration, and higher awareness. Whether teaching through synchronicities, dreams, meditative downloads, or intuitive whispers, Teacher Guides inspire your inner evolution and expansion. They remind you of the deeper meanings beneath your challenges and the sacred knowledge you carry within.

Healer Guides.

Healer Guides are compassionate, gentle energies who specialise in supporting physical, emotional, and energetic healing. They often collaborate with healers in the physical world, such as therapists, doctors, energy workers, and holistic practitioners, guiding their hands, insights, and intentions. These guides help to facilitate balance, restoration, and the release of stored pain or trauma within the body and spirit. Whether receiving healing or offering it to others, Healer Guides hold a sacred presence in the background, directing subtle energy, enhancing intuition, and bringing comfort during distress. Their presence is nurturing, and their mission is to support your return to wholeness on all levels.

Joy Guides.

Joy Guides are delightful, light-hearted beings who infuse your life with playfulness, spontaneity, and the healing power of laughter. Often experienced as childlike, whimsical, or mischievously wise, these guides help lift your vibration when life feels heavy or serious. They remind you not to lose touch with your inner child, encouraging creativity, imagination, and joyful expression. Whether it's through a sudden burst of inspiration, a perfectly timed giggle, or a serendipitous moment that warms your heart, Joy Guides help you reconnect with the simple pleasures of being alive. Their presence is a gentle reminder that joy is a sacred path to healing, connection, and spiritual alignment.

Animal Spirits.

Animal Spirits, often known as Totems or Familiars, are powerful allies from the natural world who walk beside you as protectors, messengers, and mirrors of your soul. Each animal carries symbolic wisdom, embodying traits or teachings relevant to your life path or spiritual growth. Some may appear briefly to guide you through a particular phase, while others remain with you throughout your life as a totemic presence. These spirits can help you navigate challenges, protect your energy field, and awaken dormant qualities within you. Whether they come in dreams, meditations, or repeated encounters in the physical world, Animal Spirits speak a language of instinct, intuition, and energetic resonance. They remind us that we are deeply connected to all life and that nature is a sacred guide.

Ancestral Helpers.

Ancestral Helpers are loved ones and bloodline ancestors who remain close to you from the spirit world, offering comfort, support, and healing across the generations. While they are not your assigned spirit guides, they may step forward at significant moments, mainly when you are working to break cycles, heal inherited trauma, or strengthen your connection to your roots. These ancestors often carry wisdom from their experiences, and their presence can feel familiar, grounding, and protective. They may appear in dreams, rituals, or meditations, offering messages or subtle nudges of encouragement. By working with your Ancestral Helpers, you can create powerful shifts for yourself, those who came before you and those yet to come.

Star Beings and Light Beings.

Star Beings and Light Beings are highly evolved, interdimensional entities who offer guidance, healing, and wisdom from beyond the Earthly plane. Often connected to other star systems, galaxies, or vibrational dimensions, these radiant helpers work with advanced or awakening souls on missions of planetary service, consciousness expansion, or spiritual leadership. Their energy can feel otherworldly subtle yet powerful, serene yet profound, and they often communicate through frequency, light codes, or direct downloads in altered states. Encounters with Star Beings or Light Beings may occur in dreams, meditations, or during profound spiritual experiences. They help activate soul memory, offer cosmic perspective, and assist in anchoring higher dimensional energy onto the Earth. Working with them invites profound transformation and a remembrance of your soul's galactic heritage.

Elemental or Nature Spirits.

Elemental or Nature Spirits are Earth-based energies that embody the natural world's spirit. These include faeries, devas, tree spirits, plant allies, stone beings, and the energetic consciousness of the elements of Earth, Air, Fire, Water, and Spirit. Often subtle and playful, yet deeply wise, these beings act as guardians of nature's sacred rhythms and cycles. They help ground your spiritual work, reminding you of the profound wisdom within the living Earth. When honoured with respect and reverence, Elemental Spirits may offer healing, protection, and a deeper sense of interconnectedness with all life. Working with them can awaken your senses, open your heart to nature's magic, and restore your bond with the land, the seasons, and the soul of Gaia herself.

Gatekeeper Guides.

Gatekeeper Guides are protectors of thresholds and guardians who oversee your access to spiritual realms, altered states, and higher dimensions. They regulate what energies, beings, or information may enter your consciousness during meditation, trance, astral travel, or spiritual ritual. Their role is discernment and boundary-setting, ensuring that only what serves your highest good is permitted. Gatekeepers may also guide your journey between lifetimes or watch over transitions such as births, deaths, and rebirths. When working with them, you may feel a sense of firm but loving authority as they hold the sacred space for your soul to explore safely. They are often silent and unseen, but their presence is felt when spiritual protection is needed most.

Messenger Guides.

Messenger Guides are communicators from the spirit world who deliver timely insights, signs, and intuitive nudges to help you stay aligned with your soul's path. They often appear during moments of uncertainty or decision-making, bringing clarity through synchronicities, dreams, symbols, or spontaneous thoughts. Their subtle or striking messages encourage you to listen more deeply to your inner knowing. Unlike Teacher or Guardian Guides, Messenger Guides often appear temporarily, long enough to deliver what needs to be received. They help bridge the gap between spirit and matter, translating higher wisdom into actionable guidance in your everyday life.

How Spirit Guides Communicate.

Your guides may communicate through:

Intuition.

Spirit guides often communicate through your intuition, that quiet inner knowing that arises without logical explanation. It may feel like a gut instinct, a subtle inner voice, or a sudden insight that gently nudges you in a specific direction. These intuitive whispers are your guides helping you navigate choices, avoid danger, or recognise alignment. Trusting these impressions strengthens your bond with them and fine-tunes your ability to hear their guidance more clearly.

Dreams.

Dreams are a powerful gateway for spirit guide communication. In the dreamscape, your subconscious mind is more open and receptive, allowing guides to send symbolic messages, offer healing, or even appear in complete form. These dreams may feel particularly vivid or emotionally stirring or linger in your memory long after waking. By keeping a dream journal, you may begin to recognise patterns or recurring symbols that your guides use to speak with you.

Meditation and Visualisation.

During meditation or guided visualisation, the mind enters a receptive, altered state that allows for a deeper spiritual connection. In these moments of stillness, you may see your guide in your mind's eye, hear their voice, feel their presence, or receive impressions as sensations or emotions. This is a sacred space where communication becomes more direct and clear, and it can deepen the relationship between you and your spiritual support team over time.

Automatic Writing.

Automatic writing is a form of channelling in which your guide speaks through your pen or keyboard. You may feel compelled to write without consciously planning the words in a relaxed, open state. Messages often flow quickly and with clarity, offering guidance, reassurance, or answers to questions you carry within. This practice strengthens trust in your inner voice and allows your guides to communicate in a more tangible, traceable form.

Energy Shifts.

Sometimes, your guide's presence is felt through shifts in your energetic or emotional state. You might experience a sudden wave of peace, warmth, tingling, or even a soft pressure on your shoulder or heart. These subtle sensations often arise during prayer, meditation, or moments of spiritual reflection. They are signs that your guide is near, supporting you with their calming frequency or affirming your spiritual work.

Signs and Synchronicities.

Guides often use signs and synchronicities as a playful and poetic way to get your attention. Repeated number sequences like 11:11, feathers appearing in your path, coins, rainbows, or animal encounters may all carry personal meaning. These signs often occur at the right moment, offering reassurance, guidance, or answers to questions you've been silently asking. They are spiritual breadcrumbs that remind you that you are not alone and are being guided.

Your present circumstances are the result of the seeds you have sown in the past. Your future is shaped by the choices you make today.

Paramahansa Yogananda

Meeting Your Spirit Guides.

Meeting your spirit guide is not a first encounter but a sacred remembrance, a gentle homecoming to a presence that has walked beside you since birth. These beings of light have been quietly guiding, protecting, and nudging you from the spirit realms, patiently awaiting the moment you recognise them. The connection may begin subtly: a name whispered in your mind during meditation, a vivid image in a dream, a comforting sensation of warmth during difficult times, or a sudden knowing that someone unseen is standing beside you. Your guide's energy is unique, and how you perceive them will be just as exceptional. Some experience them visually, others through sound, emotion, symbols, or energetic shifts. Building a relationship with your guide takes trust, openness, and a willingness to suspend doubt in favour of more profound listening. It is not something to force, but rather something to allow, to invite in with reverence and patience. Like any meaningful relationship, it deepens with consistent communication, respect, and shared intention. As you walk consciously with your guide, a quiet confidence grows. Daily, you'll notice a greater sense of synchronicity, clarity, and connection. Challenges may still arise, but you no longer must face them alone. Your guide becomes a trusted companion, a wise and loving presence who helps illuminate your path, especially when the future feels uncertain.

The more you open to this sacred relationship, the more you begin to understand the divine choreography of your life. Rituals, choices, and healing work take on deeper meaning when guided by a higher perspective. Whether you are making a significant life decision, performing spiritual work, or simply pausing in gratitude, the presence of your guide can be felt sometimes powerfully, sometimes subtly, but always there. Meeting your guide is a soul-affirming experience, reminding you that you are supported, loved, and deeply known across lifetimes. It is a turning point in your spiritual journey, a reminder that although we walk in human form, we are never truly walking alone. A few methods to initiate a connection include:

- Guided meditation or hypnosis to enter a receptive state where you can meet them.
- Keeping a spirit guide journal, recording intuitive impressions, dreams, and signs.
- Ask for signs aloud or in writing and be open to how those signs arrive.
- Creating an altar or sacred space honouring your guides, using candles, crystals, or objects of spiritual significance.

Why Connect with Your Spirit Team?

The more aware you are of your tribe of helpers, the more you are open to divine guidance, protection, and soul alignment. Spirit guides can:

- Help you navigate difficult choices with clarity.
- Offer healing when you're emotionally or physically drained.
- Alerts you to energy that's not aligned with your highest good.
- Support you during grief, loss, trauma, or transformation.
- Deepen your spiritual growth and awaken latent gifts.

Reflection Prompts.

1. Have you ever felt an unseen presence during a difficult time?
2. Do symbols or signs (animals, numbers, songs) repeatedly appear in your life?
3. What would you like to ask your spirit guides right now?
4. What do you imagine your leading guide looks or feels like?
5. How would your life change if you allowed yourself to be fully guided?

Exercise: Write down three signs your guides have sent you.

What is Automatic Writing?

Automatic writing, or psychography, is a powerful and intuitive practice in which you allow messages to flow through you from your subconscious mind, higher self, spirit guides, or other non-physical intelligences onto paper (or digital form) without consciously directing the words. It is a form of channelled writing in which the ego mind steps aside, and a deeper, often wiser or more spiritual voice takes over. This practice can offer healing, insight, guidance, and clarity, especially during confusion or transformation.

How It Works.

You enter a light meditative state to relax the conscious mind. Holding a pen or placing your fingers on a keyboard, you begin to write, often starting with a question or intention. The writing may begin slowly, with thoughts or symbols, then evolve into whole sentences, phrases, or profound insights. You do not judge or edit while writing. The aim is to let the words pour out freely without interference.

Where Do the Messages Come From?

Automatic writing is especially valuable for those on a spiritual path, as it bypasses logical filters and opens a channel to divine inspiration and inner truth. Depending on your spiritual beliefs and intentions, automatic writing can tap into:

Your higher self or soul wisdom.

The collective unconscious.

Spirit guides, angels, ancestors, or passed loved ones.

Divine or universal consciousness.

Common Uses of Automatic Writing:

Receiving spiritual or psychic messages.

Connecting with past lives or soul memories.

Deepening your intuition.

Accessing suppressed emotions for healing.

Gaining insight into life challenges.

Enhancing creativity or writing projects.

Communing with guides during rituals or shadow work.

How to Begin:

Set an Intention. Ask a question or seek general guidance.

Create a Sacred Space. Light a candle, ground yourself, and invite protective energies.

Enter a Meditative State. Use breathwork, sound, or visualisation.

Begin Writing Freely. No structure, no perfection, flow.

Read It Later. Let the writing rest, then return with fresh eyes to receive the message.

A Note on Discernment

Not all messages are from the highest light. Always protect your space, call in only benevolent energies, and trust your intuition to filter what is authentic and aligned.

Automatic Writing Exercise:

Set a timer for 5 minutes.

Write a letter to your spirit guide, asking for insights about a past life.

Without overthinking, write what comes to mind.

Use the writing space provided on the next page.

Our guides are extensions of ourselves. They know us better than we know ourselves because they are tuned into our soul blueprint.

Dr. Michael Newton

Exercise: Use automatic writing to ask a guide about your past life mission.

Journaling Prompts:

Describe an encounter where you felt protected by an unseen presence.

If your spirit guide could write you a message, what do you think they would say?

Dreamwork Exercise:

Before sleep, set an intention: "Spirit guides, please show me a past life memory that will help me now." Keep a dream journal to track insights.

Karma

What is Karma?

Karma is not punishment. The sacred law of cause and effect is woven into the soul's evolution. At its core, karma is a Sanskrit word meaning "action" or "deed." In spiritual traditions, karma refers to the energetic imprint of our actions, thoughts, intentions, and choices ripples we send into the universe that eventually return to us. It is the law of divine balance, a spiritual echo that returns not to punish or reward but to teach, guide, and correct. Karma holds the blueprint for learning across lifetimes, carrying lessons that the soul has not yet mastered. Karma operates on the principle that everything we do, every word we speak, every emotion we emit, and every intention we set generates energy. This energy doesn't disappear; it creates both seen and unseen effects. If our actions are rooted in love, compassion, and truth, we tend to experience peace and flow. When our actions are born of harm, fear, or betrayal, the soul may be presented with opportunities to realign, restore balance, or revisit those themes in another form. It is essential to understand that karma is not a rigid punishment system. It is a gentle teacher, a mirror held up by the universe to help us become more aware of how we shape the world and our spiritual growth. Karma often extends across multiple lifetimes. For example, unresolved conflicts, unexpressed love, or broken promises from a past life may continue to influence current relationships or personal challenges, offering us the chance to heal, forgive, and evolve. Karmic experiences can manifest in many ways:

Recurring relationship patterns.

Unexplained fears or attractions.

Lifelong emotional struggles.

Physical conditions with no clear origin.

Instant familiarity or tension with strangers.

Through soul-healing practices such as past-life regression, Akashic Records work, forgiveness rituals, and karmic release ceremonies, we can uncover the root of karmic entanglements and free ourselves from cycles that no longer serve our highest path. Ultimately, karma is not a burden but a sacred opportunity. It invites us to take responsibility for our journey and align with love, integrity, and soul truth. As we heal karma, we free ourselves and the ancestral and collective lines that similar patterns have bound.

Karma asks us:

What are you here to learn?

What are you here to give?

What are you ready to release so your soul can rise?

Unfinished Business and Karmic Debts

How Unfinished Business Carries into New Lives – Identifying Karmic Patterns

In the soul's eternal journey, not all experiences are resolved within a single lifetime. When strong emotions, broken promises, or unresolved wounds are left unhealed, they become part of the soul's energetic imprint, which we may call unfinished business. This uncompleted emotional, spiritual, or relational work doesn't disappear when the physical body dies. Instead, it is carried forward into future incarnations as part of the soul's curriculum. Unfinished business is often the result of situations that end in trauma, betrayal, guilt, injustice, or deep longing. A soul that dies with a heavy heart, unsaid words, or fractured relationships may incarnate again with the unconscious need to revisit these themes. The purpose is never punishment. Instead, it is an opportunity for completion, forgiveness, and growth.

These unresolved patterns often show up in current life as:

Recurring relationship dynamics (e.g., always attracting unavailable partners).

Unexplainable phobias or emotional sensitivities.

Instant emotional reactions to specific people or places.

Strong pulls toward particular periods or cultures.

Feelings of being stuck in repeating life challenges despite conscious effort.

This is how karma works, not as retribution but as a gentle force nudging us toward awareness, healing, and resolution. When we pay attention to the repeated themes in our lives, we begin to see the threads of karma woven through them. These patterns are like soul signposts pointing toward areas that need our love, forgiveness, or more profound understanding. Unfinished business may involve others we have known across lifetimes, karmic relationships bound by love, regret, resentment, or soul contracts. Recognising these connections can bring great clarity and peace. When we address these patterns through past life regression, inner healing work, forgiveness practices, or accessing the Akashic Records, we are healing the past and liberating the future. Completing unfinished business allows the soul to evolve, free from the weight of unresolved pain. It is a profound act of spiritual responsibility that clears the path forward and opens the heart to more profound joy, clarity, and purpose.

Our lives are but a chapter in the vast book of the soul's journey.

Dolores Cannon

Breaking free from karmic repetition – How to release cycles that no longer serve you.

Karmic repetition is the soul's way of presenting lessons that remain unintegrated; when we find ourselves facing the same struggles again and again, whether through repeated relationship patterns, emotional triggers, financial hardship, or self-sabotaging behaviour, it may be a sign that we are caught in a karmic loop. These loops are not punishments but spiritual invitations. They ask us to pause, reflect, and heal what is unresolved on a soul level. To break free from karmic repetition, awareness is the first step. Begin by identifying the themes or emotional responses that seem to echo throughout your life. Ask yourself: Where have I felt this before? What does this situation remind me of? What role do I always seem to play? Often, we find that the external details change, but the underlying feelings of abandonment, unworthiness, betrayal, and guilt remain the same. These are soul clues.

Once patterns have been brought into conscious awareness, healing can begin. Soul regression work, Akashic Records exploration, energy healing, forgiveness rituals, and inner child work all offer profound support. These practices help you retrieve the original wound, not just in this lifetime but sometimes across many, and begin to dissolve its hold over you. Breaking karmic cycles involves shifting from unconscious reaction to conscious choice. Your past does not bind you. When you become aware of a karmic pattern, you loosen its grip. The key is to respond differently to forgive instead of resent, to speak your truth rather than remain silent, to choose self-worth over people-pleasing, and to walk away when love is not returned. You may also wish to release karmic patterns through ritual formally. Writing a release letter to the soul(s) involved, cutting energetic cords, or working with affirmations such as "I now choose a new path. I release all karmic contracts that no longer serve my highest good" can be powerful tools. The karmic release is a return to sovereignty. It is a sacred act of choosing freedom over familiarity, healing over repetition. By lovingly closing these loops, you open space for new energy, soul-aligned relationships, and a future that reflects the true essence of your evolved self.

All souls, regardless of experience, are given opportunities to advance, to become more skilled, and to contribute to the growth of others.

Dr. Michael Newton, Destiny of Souls

Healing debt from past lives – Energetic ways to clear karmic imprints.

Karmic debt refers to the energetic consequences of unresolved actions or choices made in previous lifetimes, particularly those that caused harm, imbalance, or a deviation from the soul's highest truth. This "debt" is not punishment but an opportunity for balance, learning, and evolution. When we carry karmic debt, it can show up in our current life as chronic obstacles, complex relationships, unexplained guilt, limiting beliefs, or recurring emotional burdens. Often, we intuitively sense we are "carrying something" that isn't entirely born of this life. Energetic healing offers a compassionate and effective path for clearing karmic imprints. The process begins with acknowledgement, honestly reflecting on the patterns that feel heavy, cyclical, or inexplicably present. From there, healing can occur through various spiritual modalities that help release the soul from outdated contracts and emotional residue. Karmic healing does not require perfection. It requires awareness, humility, and a sincere desire to grow. When you energetically clear past life debts, you open yourself to lighter, more complementary ways of being. The burdens you carry begin to lift. Your path becomes more apparent. Most importantly, your soul returns to a state of balance, ready to move forward with clarity and grace.

Some energetic methods include:

Past–life regression Therapy involves accessing the root lifetime where the karmic wound began, experiencing the narrative, and allowing healing and forgiveness to unfold. This may include meeting the other person's soul, gaining understanding, and creating closure.

Forgiveness Rituals - Write a letter to your past self or others involved, acknowledging the pain and offering compassion. Burning or burying the letter can symbolise release.

Chakra and Aura Clearing – Energy work such as Reiki, sound healing, or crystal therapy can gently release stored karmic residue from your energy field, restoring balance and vitality.

Akashic Records Healing – In the Records, you can ask to view karmic imprints and request assistance in clearing them with the help of your spirit guides. The energy of forgiveness and grace can be invoked through prayer, intention, and guided meditation.

Affirmations and Mantras – Spoken regularly, these help rewire the subconscious mind and signal your readiness to release to the Universe. Try affirmations such as:

"I now release all karmic debt with love and gratitude."

"I honour the lessons and now choose peace and freedom."

Symbolic Acts of Service – Sometimes, karmic balance is restored through action. Engaging in conscious kindness, generosity, or helping others in areas where you once caused harm can help the soul restore harmony on an energetic level.

Ancestral and Generational Healing

Do we inherit PL trauma from our ancestors? – Exploring epigenetics and spiritual inheritance.

Ancestral and generational healing is the sacred process of addressing the unresolved pain, trauma, beliefs, and energy patterns that are passed down through family lineages energetically, emotionally, and even spiritually. Just as we inherit physical traits from our ancestors, we can also inherit their unprocessed grief, fears, and karmic burdens. These ancestral imprints can subtly influence our choices, relationships, behaviours, and even our health in this lifetime. Modern science is beginning to validate this ancient wisdom through the study of epigenetics, which explores how emotional and environmental factors can alter the expression of our genes. Traumatic experiences such as war, famine, abuse, and loss have been shown to leave biological markers on DNA, which can be passed on through multiple generations. This supports the idea that unresolved trauma does not simply disappear. It lingers in the genetic and energetic field, waiting for someone in the lineage to bring awareness, compassion, and healing. Spiritually, these inherited wounds are often described as family karma or ancestral burdens. Souls within a family may choose to incarnate again to work through collective healing, offering each other the opportunity to break cycles of dysfunction, silence, and suffering. When you feel called to heal, you are healing yourself and acting as a sacred bridge between those who came before you and those who will come after. Some signs you may be carrying ancestral or generational trauma include:

Deep-seated fears or beliefs that do not seem to originate from your life experience.

Patterns of illness, addiction, abandonment, or betrayal that run in the family.

Recurring dreams, symbols, or emotions tied to historical events or family members.

Feeling burdened, overly responsible, or strangely loyal to your lineage's suffering.

Healing these inherited wounds may involve:

- Ancestral rituals (such as lighting candles or offering prayers to the ancestors).
- Family constellation therapy works to realign ancestral relationships energetically.
- Guided meditation or hypnotherapy to connect with ancestors or access the root of the inherited pain.
- Write letters to ancestors, express forgiveness, show gratitude, and show the intention to heal the bloodline.
- Ceremonial release, where old patterns, beliefs, or burdens are symbolically returned to the earth, fire, or spirit world with reverence.

You were not randomly born into your family. If you are drawn to this work, your soul likely chose to be the one who brings light to the line. Healing ancestral trauma honours the sacrifices of those who came before you and clears the path for future generations to thrive. It is a sacred act of love, courage, and soul liberation.

Signs of ancestral burdens in your life – Recognising inherited patterns in families.

Ancestral burdens often appear as recurring patterns that echo through generations of subtle whispers of unhealed wounds, unresolved trauma, or karmic lessons passed down from your lineage. These burdens are not always visible in the form of dramatic stories or documented history; instead, they may appear as emotional undercurrents, unexplained fears, or cycles that repeat despite our efforts to break free. Spiritually speaking, ancestral burdens are energetic imprints carried within the soul's blueprint and cellular memory. They may be passed down consciously or unconsciously through the bloodline, inherited genetically, energetically, emotionally, and psychically. Recognising these signs is the first sacred step toward healing the family line and reclaiming your soul's sovereignty.

Common signs that ancestral burdens may be present in your life include:

Repetitive Emotional Patterns.

You may find yourself experiencing persistent emotions such as guilt, shame, grief, or fear that feel larger than your personal life experience would warrant. These emotions may feel ancient, familiar, and challenging to shift, suggesting they are inherited, not self-created.

Recurring Family Themes.

Noticeable themes may run through your family tree: divorce, addiction, poverty, abuse, abandonment, silence, or secrecy. You may observe similar relational or financial struggles repeated across generations, even when individual circumstances differ. These recurring themes can indicate unresolved karmic energy.

Unexplained Phobias or Health Issues.

Some phobias or chronic health issues have no known cause or logical origin but may correspond to events experienced by ancestors, such as starvation, war, or persecution. Energetically, the body may be carrying protective imprints passed down to ensure survival.

Family Silence or Taboo Subjects.

When families have unspoken traumas, unacknowledged grief, or secret histories, the energy of these experiences remains active. What is not spoken is still felt. You may notice emotional tension around specific topics or feel the presence of grief, shame, or mystery without knowing why.

Feeling Overly Responsible.

You may carry an unspoken loyalty to your lineage, feeling overly responsible for others' well-being, healing, or success. This "invisible contract" is often an ancestral burden believing that you must carry the pain of others or sacrifice your happiness to honour those who came before you.

Dreams and Visions of Ancestors or Other Time Periods.

If you frequently dream of ancestors, receive intuitive messages from deceased relatives, or feel a deep connection to times and places your family once lived, this may be a sign that you are being called to remember and heal the lineage.

You Feel Called to Do the Inner Work.

Perhaps the most telling sign of ancestral burden is that you've been called to heal. Suppose you are the first in your family to seek therapy, break the silence, follow a spiritual path, or create emotional boundaries. In that case, you are likely the cycle breaker, chosen (or volunteering) to release what your ancestors could not.

Healing ancestral burdens is a profound act of love.

As you begin this journey, remember that you are not carrying the weight alone. Your ancestors often wait in the spirit realm to support your efforts to see their stories acknowledged, their pain honoured, and their legacy transformed through your courage.

To remember who you are, you need to forget who they told you to be.

Unknown

Continue Your Soul's Journey with Me

If this book has stirred something within you, know this is just the beginning. As a qualified Hypnotherapist, Regression Therapist, CBT Practitioner, and Spiritual Coach, I offer one-to-one sessions and teachings to support your healing, insight, and spiritual growth. Sessions can be run in person or via Zoom.

Offerings Include:

Past Life Regression

Life Between Lives Spiritual Regression

Future Life Progression

Spirit Release Therapy

Hypnotherapy

Inner Child Healing

Spiritual Life Coaching

Spiritual Talking Group

Training:

Psychic Development (Zoom)

Hypnotherapy Training

Advanced Hypnotherapy Training

Diploma in Regression Therapy Training

Each session is tailored with care, intuition, and experience to help you reconnect with your soul's truth, heal deeply, and awaken your inner wisdom.

Learn more, book a session, or explore my online teachings at:

www.lifecycletherapies.com

https://www.youtube.com/@lifecycletherapies/playlists

lifecycletherapies@hotmail.com

https://www.instagram.com/lifecycletherapies

https://www.facebook.com/lifecycletherapies

Life Cycle THERAPIES

Other books by this Author

Reconnecting with Your Inner Child – A Workbook for Self-Healing

Reconnecting with Your Inner Child is a gentle yet powerful guide for anyone longing to heal emotional wounds, release the past, and rediscover the joy, creativity, and innocence within. This workbook invites you to build a loving relationship with your younger self through reflective exercises, therapeutic journaling prompts, and heart-opening practices. Whether you're beginning your healing journey or deepening your personal growth, this soulful companion helps uncover buried emotions, transform limiting patterns, and restore a sense of wholeness. Compassionately written and spiritually grounded, it offers a safe space to reconnect with the child you once were and to nurture the adult you are becoming.

Chakra Healing - A Workbook for Self-Healing

Chakra Healing is a transformative journey through the body's energy centres, offering practical tools for balancing, activating, and aligning your chakra system. Blending ancient wisdom with modern spiritual practice, this workbook guides you through each of the seven primary chakras with insightful teachings, colour psychology, crystal recommendations, affirmations, meditations, and journaling prompts. Whether new to energy healing or deepening your spiritual path, this beautifully structured guide empowers you to clear energetic blockages, awaken inner harmony, and reclaim your power. Step into alignment, elevate your frequency, and master your energy from root to crown.

Trance and Transformation - A Workbook for Self-Healing

Step into the sacred space of your subconscious and awaken the healer within. *Trance and Transformation* is a profoundly spiritual and practical guide to the natural power of hypnotherapy, self-hypnosis, and meditation. Blending science, soul, and storytelling, this transformative workbook gently demystifies the art of trance while offering profound tools for healing, reprogramming, and spiritual growth. Discover the pioneers who paved the way, explore hypnotic states, and learn to harness the subconscious mind for lasting change. A must-have companion for seekers, therapists, and anyone longing to reconnect with the wisdom of the inner self. Whether you're a curious beginner or a seasoned seeker, this book invites you to explore altered states of awareness for profound personal evolution and lasting change.

Auras and Energy Bodies – A Workbook for Self-Healing

This workbook is a gentle, practical guide to understanding your energetic anatomy and reclaiming your spiritual strength. Explore the layers of your energy body, uncover the meaning behind aura colours, and learn how to cleanse, balance, and protect your field with intuitive and accessible techniques. Whether you're a sensitive soul, an empath, a healer, or a spiritual seeker, this workbook offers simple yet powerful tools for emotional resilience, psychic shielding, and energetic sovereignty. Let this sacred companion support you in building firm boundaries, restoring inner clarity, and walking your path with confidence, awareness, and light.

Past Life Regression – A Workbook for Self-Healing

Step beyond the present moment's veil and into the soul's timeless landscapes. Healing through *Past Life Regression* invites you on a profound journey of remembrance and release, guiding you to uncover the echoes of who you've been to heal who you are today. Written for the curious, the seekers, and those who sense there is more to life than meets the eye, this book offers a gentle yet powerful introduction to the transformative world of regression therapy. Whether preparing for your first regression session, exploring your healing path, or simply curious about the soul's journey across lifetimes, this book will meet you where you are and walk beside you toward clarity, freedom, and renewal. Your soul remembers. Are you ready to listen?

Energy Protection – A Workbook on Self-Healing

This deeply supportive workbook is a sacred guide for anyone who gives from the heart, holds space for others, or walks the path of spiritual service. You know that energy matters whether you are a therapist, healer, intuitive, carer, or sensitive soul. And you may have felt the quiet exhaustion, emotional heaviness, or spiritual depletion when your energy is unguarded. *Energy Protection* offers a grounded, compassionate, and empowering approach to restoring energy clarity, strength, and sovereignty. Through accessible teachings, reflection prompts, and practical tools, this workbook helps you identify where and why your energy leaks and then shows you how to gently and powerfully restore your boundaries, vitality, and inner peace.

Inside, you'll explore:

– The true nature of personal energy and why it becomes depleted.

– Emotional absorption, spiritual overexposure, and unconscious agreements.

– Burnout, compassion fatigue, and collective overwhelm.

– How to protect, maintain, and cleanse your energy daily.

– Practical rituals, energetic "first aid," and long-term self-repair.

– A return to soul integrity and empowered service.

Printed in Great Britain
by Amazon

61084250R00067